Perspectives in Reading No. 13

READING AND REVOLUTION: The Role of Reading in Today's Society

Compiled and Edited by

DOROTHY M. DIETRICH
Uniondale, New York, Public Schools

and

VIRGINIA H. MATHEWS
Association of American Publishers

Prepared by the Joint Committee on Reading Development of the
International Reading Association

and

Association of American Publishers

INTERNATIONAL READING ASSOCIATION
Newark, Delaware 19711

INTERNATIONAL READING ASSOCIATION

OFFICERS

1970-1971

President	DONALD L. CLELAND, University of Pittsburgh, Pittsburgh, Pennsylvania
President-elect	THEODORE L. HARRIS, University of Puget Sound, Tacoma, Washington
Past President	HELEN HUUS, University of Missouri, Kansas City, Missouri

DIRECTORS

Term expiring Spring 1971

William K. Durr, Michigan State University, East Lansing, Michigan
Mildred H. Freeman, Urban Laboratory in Education, Atlanta, Georgia
Ethel M. King, University of Calgary, Calgary, Alberta

Term expiring Spring 1972

Thomas C. Barrett, University of Wisconsin, Madison, Wisconsin
Constance M. McCullough, San Francisco State College, San Francisco, California
Eileen E. Sargent, Nicolet Union High School, Milwaukee, Wisconsin

Term expiring Spring 1973

Marjorie S. Johnson, Temple University, Philadelphia, Pennsylvania
Robert Karlin, Queens College, City University of New York, Flushing, New York
Olive S. Niles, State Department of Education, Hartford, Connecticut

---

Executive Secretary-Treasurer	RALPH C. STAIGER, University of Delaware, Newark, Delaware
Assistant Executive Secretary	RONALD W. MITCHELL, International Reading Association, Newark, Delaware
Publications Coordinator	FAYE R. BRANCA, International Reading Association, Newark, Delaware

---

Contents

Foreword

THE PERSPECTIVE CONFERENCES of the International Reading Association are conceived as forums where topics and issues can be thoroughly discussed. Often these conferences are jointly sponsored with other groups and are held in connection with conventions of other professional associations. The conference on "Reading and Revolution: The Role of Reading in Today's Society" was jointly sponsored by the International Reading Association and the Association of American Publishers. Dorothy M. Dietrich and Virginia H. Mathews planned and directed the conference which was held in Chicago, March 14-15, 1969, as an ASCD preconvention activity.

The cochairmen were determined that the conference would present the viewpoints of various specialists. The success of this decision is manifest in the program, the papers, and the discussion. In spite of the diversity in background of the speakers and the range of topics discussed, certain themes emerged from the conference:

- Literacy will continue to be a prime prerequisite for successful citizenship in our society. Manpower trends suggest that higher levels of literacy will be required in the future.
- Teaching and learning to read are not restricted to the school. The home, industry, and other agencies play a role, too.
- The paraprofessional and the volunteer tutor are of growing significance for providing the support to the school's effort that traditionally was provided by the home. Changing social conditions have made this new human resource a valuable addition to the range of resources available to the school.
- Children can be helped to learn better through organized preschool experiences. Social realities have increased the need for these experiences for growing proportions of our children.
- Literacy is not only a matter of skills. A literate person is one who, in fact, reads; otherwise, there is no advantage in possessing the ability to read. Content, therefore, becomes an important factor in developing the habit of reading for personal development.

Much food for thought is found in the various papers and in the recorded discussions all of which relate to the role of reading in our changing society. The conference stands as a tribute to the insightful planning of the cochairmen.

LEO FAY
Indiana University

Introduction

A TIME OF EXPONENTIAL CHANGE is not a time to take anything for granted. It is a time to question, to reassess the value of institutions and methods, and (if they meet the test) to reaffirm their value in terms of the new order.

As a group of professionals concerned with reading motivation and methods, we met to test the assumption that reading remains the basic communications skill essential to releasing and training human potential— an instructional priority. We found the assumption valid, and the pages that follow give many reasons why the ability to read is what parents of all classes want for their children; what employers seek in their employees; and what people of all ages use to help stabilize their world, shape their self-identity, and give meaning, pleasure, and style, to learning and leisure.

Also, in the pages that follow are leads, suggestions, and mandates: to teachers and parents, to professionals and laymen, to associations and agencies. To motivate children to read we must both expose them to credible people and introduce them to things to know and wonder about. In order to follow up the teaching of skills and motivation, we must provide access to a rich variety of books from which to choose and read. It is a big job, but worth the effort, and it is our hope that this book will lend some small measure of encouragement and reinforcement.

D.M.D.
V.H.M.

Contributors

Norman Bradburn
National Opinion Research Center
Chicago, Illinois

Margaret Burroughs
Director, DuSable Museum of
African-American History
Chicago, Illinois

Audrey C. Cohen
Women's Talent Corps/
College for Human Services
New York, New York

Dorothy Dietrich
District Supervisor of Reading
Uniondale, New York

Philip H. Ennis
Professor of Sociology
Wesleyan University

Leo Fay
Professor of Education
Indiana University

Marion Henley
Chicago Urban League
Chicago, Illinois

Robert D. Johnson
Westinghouse Learning Corporation
Edinburg, Indiana

James W. Mann
Associate Professor of Education
Roosevelt University

Virginia H. Mathews
Association of American Publishers
New York, New York

Omar K. Moore
Professor of Social Psychology
University of Pittsburgh

Harry O. Patterson
General Motors Institute
Flint, Michigan

Nancy Ponsonby
Reading Consultant
Oak Park, Illinois, Elementary Schools

Roman C. Pucinski
U.S. House of Representatives
Washington, D.C.

Otho Robinson
District Superintendent 20
Chicago, Illinois, Public Schools

Philip J. Rutledge
Stanley H. Ruttenberg & Associates
Washington, D.C.

Henry Springs
Principal, Marshall High School
Chicago, Illinois

Samuel Stratton
Afro-American Round Table
Chicago, Illinois

Catherine E. White
EDL/McGraw-Hill Book Company
Huntington, New York

The International Reading Association attempts, through its publications, to provide a forum for a wide spectrum of opinion on reading. This policy permits divergent viewpoints without assuming the endorsement of the Association.

The Relevance of Reading to the Social Revolution

James W. Mann

IT HAS BEEN a long time since the young woman in the ad for Virginia Slims cigarettes was caught smoking behind the fruit shelves in the basement and, consequently, sent straight to bed by her husband. There have been some other changes, too, since then, and it is with these other changes that we are concerned in our discussion. In fact, the changes we are now experiencing are so numerous, so rapid, and so diverse that they almost defy organization or interpretation. There is no tidy definition of the social revolution as I see it today; it is a welter of ideas, words, feelings, actions, and reactions—all characterized by divergency and a lack of clearly defined goals. The emphasis seems negative. The one persistent characteristic of our present condition is constant change.

This discussion should begin with a definitive statement and a scholarly treatment of the social revolution. Not being a sociologist, I shall avoid the difficult task of definition and try another means of establishing a base for our deliberations.

As I thought of the topic and particularly of the word *relevant,* I began to jot down all the words, phrases, impressions, and ideas which surround and engulf us today. As I developed this material, I began to see it clearly as sort of a deluge of undigested ideas and impressions. Frankly, I found that I had created a sort of monster, and, as an educator, was frightened at the implications.

So, for what it is worth, here is Exhibit: The Social Revolution or, to rephrase it, Exhibit: The "Now Environment."

EXHIBIT: THE NEW "NOW" ENVIRONMENT

CHANGE:
Family; Church; Community; School
The Population Explosion
The Establishment; Anti-Establishment; In; Out

ECONOMICS:
Affluence; Poverty
Class; Status
Blue Collar; White Collar
Mobility; Transiency

PEOPLE:
Mods; Squares; Hippies; Yippies
Flower People; the Guru
White People; Black People; Whitey
The Fuzz; The Law; Pigs

RACE:
Segregation; Integration; Separation
Racists; WASPS; Red Necks
Moderates; Militants

PROTEST:
Marches; Sit Ins; Rap Ins; Sit Downs; Lie Downs; Probe In; Confrontation; Demands; The Crunch
Concerned Parents; Concerned Property Owners; Concerned. . .
Involvement; Noninvolvement; Turned Off; Turned On
Dropouts; Drop Ins; Cop Outs

POWER:
"Revolution—Not Evolution"
White Power; Black Power; Teacher Power; Pupil Power
Violence; Destruction; Brutality; "Burn, Baby, Burn"
Back Lash; White Lash; Black Lash

GAPS:
The Generation Gap; The Communications Gap; The Credibility Gap
The Teacher-Pupil Gap; The Teacher-Parent Gap
The Teacher-Administration Gap
Freak Out; Psyche Out

COMMUNICATION-
EXPRESSION:
The New Freedom; Freedom of Expression; Censorship
The Underground Press; Free Press; Student Press
Graffiti; Obscenity; Pornography
The Living Theater; The "Now" Movie
Concrete Poetry; Avante-Garde Art; Soul Music
Love; Soul; Black is Beautiful; Simpatico
Sex; Pot; LSD; A Trip; Blow My Mind
"Telling it like it is"

CAUSES:
Peace; War; The Draft; The Bomb
Hawks; Doves
Law and Order; Punishment
Capital Punishment; Euthanasia
Reform; Repress; Revert; Protect

(All items subject to change without notice)

This exhibit is a frightening collection of impressions; if we can accept it as fairly describing our present condition, then the social revolution is more an environment than a movement. Lacking cohesion and defined purpose, the revolution substitutes a sort of wild and irresponsible excitement. For young people it can be overwhelming, confusing, tempting, and frightening. But for now, it is pretty much their world, and it absorbs most of their energy and their attention.

Consider one revolution, that in the mass media—publishing, films, television, the theatre and the arts. This is a revolution both in content and in techniques; it is spectacular and compelling. Consider, for example, the effect of the new films, the "now movies." The *Saturday Review* of December 28, 1968, contains an article which I highly recommend by Anthony Schillaci on the "now movie." The author writes from his experience at Fordham University where he teaches contemporary film, stages film festivals, and surveys student opinions. I quote from his article, "Films as Environment."

> The effect of such films (e.g. *The Graduate, Bonnie and Clyde, Rosemary's Baby, Flicker*) is a series of open-ended impressions, freely evoked and enjoyed, strongly inviting inquiry and involvement. In short, film is freed to work as environment, something which does not simply contain, but shapes people—tilting the balance of their faculties, radically altering their perceptions, and ultimately their views of self and all reality. Perhaps one sense of the symptomatic word "grooving," which applies to both sight and sound environment, is that a new mode of attention—multisensory, total, and simultaneous—has arrived. When you groove, you do not analyze, follow an argument, or separate sensations; rather you are massaged into feelings of heightened life and consciousness.

There are challenging, even frightening, implications in what Father Schillaci is saying. In relation to the traditional school environment and content, the "now movie" is formidable competition for the attention of our youth. The influence of what we offer in school is certainly no match for the impact of the films of today, or other aspects of the "now" environment. We must somehow deal with this competition and hope to close the gap between in-school learning and this all-compelling, out-of-school environment.

Recently I have been observing classes in a junior high school. At one time I taught in a junior high school and enjoyed the experience. Now I wonder whether I could muster the patience, wisdom, and proper degree of sophistication to cope with the youngsters. I was fascinated by their facility in their choice of involvement. At one moment they "turned off" completely; at the next they hurled themselves into the discussion. One boy picked up a word from the instructor, turned the word into a completely irrelevant double-entendre, and tossed it to his friends amid laughter and snickering. He had managed to bring a bit of his own environment into the classroom.

Typically and traditionally, schools are engaged in presenting worthwhile content in preparation for future needs of the individual and of society. This is our stated mission. We teach "problem solving," "critical thinking," "intelligent evaluation." All of us know the problem here. If these exercises have no real relevance for our students, we have labored in vain. Even the goal of "process" learning is limited by its relevance. Relevance is subject to pupil acceptance, and this is the heart of the problem so far as teaching and school learning are involved. It is a central question for us. Given the school as it is today, can we hope to achieve the kind of relevance which has meaning for our students? To achieve relevance, must we give up too much? Is the new environment all bad? Is the social revolution capable of producing new values? To lend some perspective and a hopeful note, I refer again to Father Schillaci. He quotes one of his students as saying that the reason the fellows take their girls to these movies is to have "something important to talk about." He suggests that "film is a creative agent in change" and says further, "Education increasingly means developing the ability to live humanly in the technological culture by changing with it."

At this point we should move to the question of reading and its relevancy to the social revolution. I have suggested that the usual school offerings pose problems of relevancy. Now, can reading be an agent of reconciliation between school and out-of-school learning? Let us review our position as to the basic purposes of reading. Jeanne Chall, in *Learning to Read: The Great Debate,* outlines what she terms a consensus of sorts among reading experts since the 1930's:

> The purpose of reading should be defined broadly to include as major goals right from the start, not only word recognition, but also comprehension and interpretation, appreciation, and application of what is read to the study of personal and social problems.

I am sure that we can subscribe to the goals of comprehension, interpretation, and appreciation. I want to emphasize particularly the words *application of what is read to the study of personal and social problems.* There is no question that young people today are confused and uncertain about themselves and their future. We can safely assume that they are seeking answers beyond those given them in classes. For example, students are taking fewer books from the libraries (causing concern among librarians), but they are crowding the racks to buy paperbacks for themselves. Here there is a wide selection of material, much of it relating to the new and the "now" environment. The principle of self-selection is a potent factor. But, as to how the young interpret this phenomena, who knows what is happening, except perhaps that the gap is widening between the students and the establishment. Some teachers might even be amazed to find that students are reading at all, based on their performance in school. William H. Glass in *Omensetter's Luck* tells of his experience with reading: "I was a very slow reader, making a sudden breakthrough in about fifth grade. I don't understand because, although I was reading very badly in school, at home I was reading Mallory in the old English. I don't know why."

As a possible function of reading as it operates to fulfill the goals set down by Chall, suppose that we find out what young people are reading. Let us read it ourselves. Then, let us open our classes to discussion and interpretation of the ideas and points of view expressed in this material. Relevance to adults means what is generally pertinent. But young people ask, "Pertinent to what? How does it concern us?" By free and open discussion, we can help students acquire understanding and perspective on questions that concern them. This to them is relevancy, and this they can accept.

Can we assume, then, that one bridge between school learning and the environment of students is the acceptance of student-selected content (reading) as educationally valid and productive for the students? I believe that we can accept it and, perhaps, must if we are to maintain the school as an effective institution. One caution must be observed, one that may seem like a weak concession to keep our students with us and to avoid the so-called question of value conflicts. Actually, there is evidence that our youth do not really want us to become like them. The anxious mother who dons miniskirts to promote understanding with her teenage daughter causes only embarrassment. The quest for understanding is part of the search for new values which youth can accept, even though these values may turn out to be not really too different from those of their elders. Good teaching can help students to accomplish this quest. This understanding may actually be more a necessity than a risk, but we are "up tight" on the subject and must respond in some meaningful way.

I do not propose to blueprint a program or to prescribe detailed plans. I have no bag of tricks, and I would be loath to present them if I had. I would rather every teacher work creatively and resourcefully to develop a program with her pupils. Each of us must do his own research and find his own answers and thereby open the door to new content and new procedures. We must be prepared to examine freely and frankly, without sham and hypocrisy, all the ideas and opinions that our students present and, in this way, hopefully, help them find their own directions. The difference between the fellows who "take their girls to the movies to have something serious to talk about" and the elderly matron who complained that *Bonnie and Clyde* was a bad movie "because it taught bad driving habits," exposes both the generation gap and a relevancy gap.

William Van Till, in *Today's Education* (December 1968), suggests three alternatives for curriculum: 1) change the content from the irrelevant to the relevant; 2) if unable to change the content, teach it in such a way as to give it relevance; and 3) continue with meaningless content, break one's heart trying to teach, and achieve very little. Most schools, although by no means all, have abandoned the third alternative. There are notable examples of teachers who are making progress toward success with the second. Instances of the first alternative are few.

The idea of moving out of the present framework of curriculum and content into one of greater relevancy is perhaps the most hopeful, given the present framework of attitudes among our students. Attacking the problem through reading has merit and potential. Through reading, we can open up a wider range of content without seriously upsetting established tradition.

Another area of concern is the idea that reading is an end in itself. We seem to teach it as a *subject* of the curriculum instead of as a *function* which illuminates all facets of learning and of life itself. The reading text, if it serves its true purpose, should phase itself out relatively early in the school program. The separate periods for reading instruction should continue only to serve those who need to strengthen their skills and eliminate defects which hamper progress. At the same time others are freed to use reading functionally. I am disturbed by the belief, implied or stated, that reading is a *prerequisite* to learning. Parents and lay persons hold this belief; teachers practice it, often as a policy of the school. This approach leads to a condition that is self-defeating and restrictive. It is further believed, and implemented in practice, that other learnings must wait until the requisite skills are mastered. This practice is not really valid. We know that children are learning even before they talk. They learn before they come to school. And when they are in school, they are learning—developing concepts and learning facts and processes without benefit of reading. For example, it is generally found that children in the ghetto have arithmetic achievement beyond their reading levels. I would suggest that learning in other areas could be fostered as a means of motivating reading and of helping children move ahead and gain momentum.

In school-after-school, the morning is devoted to reading classes which, on occasion, are extended into the afternoon. In addition, the intensity of teaching increases in proportion to the need, and those who read most poorly must "work that much harder." To add a measure of insult to injury, a federal program in reading is provided after school, where tired (and often untrained teachers) attempt to teach reading to tired and hungry children. The effect on children's attitudes toward reading is obvious. Further complicating the situation is the belief among some educators (and noneducators) that the fault lies in the methods used. So the pressure is on for an all-out attempt to find *a method* and to narrow the approach to specially structured methods such as alphabetic, phonetic, code, or linguistic. In one school, for example, I found all teachers teaching reading through a linguistic approach, and I found that they had been instructed to use no other method. If viewed in the total perspective, the elements of method techniques, timing, and methodology should *supplement* the ultimate purposes of reading, not *supplant* them.

On the brighter side, there are schools and teachers who are teaching and using reading in ways that bring about significant relevancy. To acknowledge a selected few and to point to a hopeful trend, I offer the following:

- In a vocational guidance school in Chicago, teenage students were attentively reading *Rules of the Road,* the official document of the state highway department, in preparation for taking the driver's test.
- A high school boy brought home a book of poetry from his English class. It was *Reflections on the Gift of a Watermelon Pickle.* His mother reported that the material had both relevance and merit, and the son approved highly of the content.
- Literature classes draw parallels between situations in the classics and modern life and writings.
- Programs provide paperback books to children in school through book clubs, mobile book shelves, and other means to encourage personal ownership and self-selection of books.
- Teachers become involved with children in discussion and evaluation of plays, movies, and television programs which occur outside of school.
- Acknowledge the power of mass media by using it in school in conjunction with reading. A children's librarian experiments with "mixing of media" with story telling to "stimulate new ideas and to relate ideas from the stories to contemporary experience." Another librarian points out that in 1968 stories about crime, dope, and gangs are "less shocking than they seemed to be in 1930."
- A teacher in a ghetto school uses several rope jumping patterns, dictated by the children from their own experiences, as experience charts in beginning reading. (They were nonreaders at the second grade level but made rapid progress with the material.)
- An elementary school in Chicago has experimented with ministories taken verbatim from kindergarten children and transcribed them onto experience charts for beginning reading in grade one. (Relevancy was established through content, indigenous vocabulary, and language patterns.)
- Using a child's dictated stories as his personal reading material is an element of individualized reading which is relevant and effective.

- "Drop In" schools for school dropouts apply the principle of self-selection and self-motivation as a basis for their programs.
- According to Arnold Gingrich, publisher of *Esquire Magazine,* readers today are looking to periodicals for in-depth and interpretative treatment of current problems. The daily press is also catering to this need.
- An English teacher, concerned with the gap between student talk and school talk had her class develop a "hiptionary" which listed "in" vocabulary words and defined them in correct English terms.

In summary, I reiterate some of my major concerns and proposals:

1. That we maintain confidence in comprehension, interpretation, appreciation, and application of what is being read as the basic goals in reading and give them priority in teaching.
2. That techniques and methodology be made to serve these ends and that they not be held primary in emphasis or in timing.
3. That we exploit to the fullest the value of individual personal motivation through a sense of involvement in content.
4. That we face the fact that relevance to students is more closely related to the now environment than it is to the traditional school content.

One final thought: with the mass of research and resulting theories in the field of reading, it would seem that we should be well along the road to success in the teaching of reading; from my personal observations and experience, I detect an area of weakness in our current approach and offer a possible direction.

I believe that our ability to implement the information and know-how that exist in the field of reading instruction breaks down at the teaching level—in the classroom. It breaks down through lack of supervision, particularly at the beginning level, and through pressures put upon the teachers for early results. The presssures, coming from parents, community, and school administration, cause the teacher to grasp for a panacea, which inhibits good teaching and discourages a broad approach. There is not enough time for teachers to survey the field and select multiple approaches appropriate to a particular group in a particular setting. Adequate supervisory programs and materials resources could correct this weakness by reducing pressures and allowing maximum use of teacher talent. I strongly advocate cooperative efforts with heavy emphasis on inservice education and supervision and strong support, assistance, and direction for the classroom teacher. To win this battle for adequate reading, don't deposit the ammunition short of the firing line; carry it to the embattled soldier, the classroom teacher.

The Relevance of Reading to the Technological Revolution

Philip J. Rutledge

MORE THAN A FEW of us can trace our origins to someone who once made his way in this country by manual labor—as a mule skinner, a sandhog, a gandy dancer, or, in my case, a cotton picker. The mule skinner, gandy dancer, and cotton picker are long gone, and the sandhog is on his way out. Future generations will say, "My father, or my grandfather, was an astronaut, or a cytotechnologist, or a computer programer"—or a member of some new profession requiring as yet undefined skills.

The point here is that both the country and the jobs that keep it running have undergone rapid changes in recent years. A study of future manpower needs by the Battelle Institute brings into sharp focus the relevance of reading to this technological revolution. The Battelle Report concludes that "Recent changes in the national economy indicate that the socioeconomic structure is evolving into what might be called the human resources era." Broadly speaking, the evolution of the United States economy can be described in terms of three distinguishable historical periods:

- The Agricultural Era, which ended in the late 1800s.
- The Manufacturing Era, which lasted through the late 1950s.
- The Human Resources Era, which emerged during the early 1960s.

In the emerging human resources era, the Battelle Report predicts that

. . . the economy will find its essential vitality in those activities which are related to the unique resources of man—namely, his brain, which is

9

the source of the creative adaptive potentials required by our increasing technological sophistication. Contrasted with the agricultural and manufacturing eras when most workers were concerned primarily with transforming natural resources into useful products for their fellowman—activities which generally involved physical dexterity or strength—a rapidly increasing number of workers in the human resources era will need a high level of educational achievement and mental development to meet job requirements.

Manpower experts tell us, however, that the number of persons attaining that "high level of educational achievement and mental development" is just not enough to meet our nation's needs even today—and certainly not tomorrow! Too many workers—hampered by lack of skill, inadequate schooling, and poor work history—are coming to the job market unprepared; and far too many more, after a series of brief, unsuccessful encounters in the world of work, are dropping out altogether. Those failing to acquire skill in reading are destined to become casualties of the technological revolution.

Before we can address ourselves to the issue of reading and its relevance, it is necessary to gain some insight into the character of the technological revolution. In view of the fact that we are probably still in the midst of that revolution and, therefore, lack the perspective of history, any attempt to define parameters will have to be tenuous. Scholars are still attempting to gain insights into the nature of this technological change.

Harvard University published the fourth annual report of its special Program on Technology and Society, established by a grant from the IBM Corporation to "undertake an inquiry in depth into the effects of technological change on the economy, on public policies, and on the character of society, as well as into the reciprocal effects of social progress on the nature, dimension, and directions of scientific and technological developments." This annual report is well worth reading.

In one sense, the technological revolution began with, and has continued since, the invention of the wheel. But this is really too broad a view for our purposes. The industrial and social changes stimulated by the advent of the manufacturing era a hundred or so years ago may be closer to the demarcation point. Its chief characteristics were the development of large scale mass production of goods and the accompanying specialization and differentiation of job structures. The social, political, and economic significance of the industrial revolution was tremendous, as we are well aware. It was the major impetus to the formation of the urban society with its intrinsic characteristics: large dense agglomerations of people; political fragmentation; urban sprawl; subsequent deterioration of the core; problems of poverty; and so on. However, the industrial revolution did not, by these intrinsic qualities, spur on a greater need for reading ability. The types of jobs it created—highly specialized, repetitive ones—did not require of people the ability to communicate effectively in various ways.

It is the post-industrial age—the age of the automobile, the airplane, the computer, the satellite, and the spaceship—that has made reading and writing ability a necessity. This post-industrial age might best be labelled the mass media era, or the communications and information systems era, or perhaps, the *cybernetic era,* instead of the human resources era.

Cybernetics is a science inspired by and having a basis in the study of nature's own automatic control system—the nervous system and the brain. From this study, mechanical-electrical communications systems have been developed as extensions of the human brain and sensory system allowing us to acquire, have access to, and utilize massive amounts of information.

The nature of this technological revolution has become more sophisticated than the average person knows. There are now communication and control systems of astounding proportions. We have machines which run entire factories without the use of human hands. The technique called autofacturing implies utilization of machines which manufacture other machines, with only a human computer operator to supervise. Meanwhile, the work week is being reduced, so that in our lifetimes we can look forward to such amounts of leisure time that *its* use will become the problem, rather than the use of working time.

The consequence is that skill has replaced property as the primary economic value and as the prime determinant of social status. The human resources era or cybernetic era is characterized by extensive geographic and social mobility for the individual with skills, especially communications skills of various types, including and emphasizing the ability to communicate with machines. This mobility is the result of the combined effect of specialization, plus the socioeconomic interdependence of the urban society, plus the revolution in communications and transportation technology. By the year 2000, it has been predicted that persons will move about the world in pursuit of a career as some of us now move about the United States.

The ability to communicate through the use of some symbolically based method—language whether written or spoken, whether logic or mathematics—is absolutely essential. It is essential because of the necessity to preserve, retrieve, use, and convey the tremendous amounts of knowledge accumulating with constantly increasing rapidity in the physical, natural, and social sciences. It is also essential because our technology has advanced to the stage at which machines are doing more and more of the specialized, routine, and monotonous tasks formerly done by human workers. With this freeing of workers for more challenging and complex tasks, notably the running of the machines themselves, the necessity to communicate and to understand communications with a high degree of preciseness has been accelerated to a degree, and at a pace, without precedent.

What does all this mean for the expanding economy produced by the current technological revolution? What does it mean for the labor force required to man such an economy? Particularly, what does it mean for the youth of our country, some one million of whom either dropped out or were pushed out of the educational system before completing high school this year alone?

Official studies of the U. S. Department of Labor have indicated that those occupations in which the highest percentage of growth is anticipated are those concentrated at the upper end of the skill ladder, where formal training is most important. It is projected, for example, that the need for professional and technical workers—computer technicians, scientists, engineers, teachers, health personnel, social service workers—will show an increase of over 40 percent between 1965 and 1975, reaching a total of 13 million by 1975. This is an increase twice that of all other occupations.

Compounding the effects of these figures on the employment market is the number of college and postgraduate degree holders projected by the U. S. Office of Education. Between 1966 and 1975 it is anticipated that the number of M.A. and Ph.D. degrees will double, while the number of A.B. degrees awarded by colleges and universities will increase by two-thirds.

The conclusion which one must draw from these data is that professional and technical expertise, in the words of the President's Manpower Report, ". . . has been both a cause and a consequence of this country's advancing economy and technology." While our rapid pace of scientific discovery and technological innovation has been the achievement of scientists and engineers, it has, in a self-perpetuating process, also created an overwhelming demand for the services of these professionals and for the upgrading of supportive occupations. When considered in terms of further data on educational achievement and occupational attainment levels, these observations have significant implications for an overwhelming portion of our population.

In a survey published by *Fortune* magazine, dropout records were cited for that student population which had reached the age of 17 at the time of the 1960 census and who in 1975 at age 32 would be expected to be part of the prime reservoir of leadership talent for our national purpose. The survey included entrance and completion stages between grade school and graduate study. Seven percent of those youngsters entering grade school failed to enter high school. Though this figure is not inordinately high when various attending factors are taken into consideration, the figures beyond this elementary level do take on increasingly startling proportions. Of those entering high school (2,662,000), 30 percent did not graduate. Fifty percent of those who completed high school failed to continue their education; and of those who did enter college (923,000), 50.4 percent did not finish a four-year program. Slightly less than 25 percent of college graduates proceeded to the graduate level.

Equally significant is statistical evidence for the 25-29 age group, male only, of occupation by educational level. At the extremes: 75 percent of those positions categorized as *professional, technician, manager, official,* and *proprietor,* were filled by men with four or more years of college, while only 15 percent of these positions were held by high school graduates, with 5.5 percent held by those who failed to complete high school. The largest percentage (approximately 62 percent of those who lacked a high school diploma were classified as *semiskilled, labor,* and *service workers.*

And here we begin to see even more clearly the relevance of reading to the technological revolution as we enter the cybernetic or human resources era. In this era we must begin to concentrate on the effective development of human beings. Such effective development will have to include training which will allow individuals to use our technology in an optimal way.

Intellectual obsolescence will be the common destiny of 11 million people in this country, 18 years or over, who have not completed fifth grade, of 25 million who have not completed eighth grade, and of 58 million people who have not completed high school unless we somehow motivate them to acquire new reading skills. Although these figures include all age groups, there are two million adults in the 18-24 year bracket who have less than eight years of schooling.

Our country faces an economy in which advancing technology is rapidly eliminating occupations which traditionally absorbed the undereducated. In 1900, two out of every three employed persons worked with their hands. Today, the primary skills of the undereducated—those motor skills which were the mainstay of the manufacturing era—are giving way to the intellectual and communications skills of the cybernetic era.

What—in an environment so described—becomes of those who cannot read sufficiently to improve or update their skills, who do not possess a basic literacy level that meets minimum standards for government retraining programs or industry-sponsored on-the-job training programs, and who are not equipped to identify sources of job opportunities or to combat discriminatory hiring practices?

A Federal Interagency Manpower Planning Task Force estimates that there are 11 million persons in our nation who are chronically in poverty and for whom better employment is a possible solution to their own poverty and the poverty of their dependents. Perhaps two-thirds or about seven million persons possess inadequate education and training for the skills required in today's job market. These are the persons who make up the majority of "the disadvantaged" about whom we are concerned.

There are several definitions of the disadvantaged, and an instructive profile has emerged from the thousands of persons who participated in the job training programs of the Department of Labor. Typically, the disadvantaged person

- has a sixth grade education or equivalent, with extremely poor verbal skills;
- has never received intensive skill training;
- had parents who were also unskilled;
- has been unemployed for 17 months;
- lives with one and one-half families;
- needs eye glasses, dental work;
- has seen a physician only once in his life;
- is married with three children;
- has no transportation;
- has had some contact with the law and has spent at least 30 days in jail.

A number of approaches to helping the nonreading disadvantaged in our cities might be taken; many have been suggested. At the heart of this problem, however, is the need for our public schools to do a better job of educating and training young people for the types of jobs needed in our expanding economy.

Serious questions, however, have been raised as to the ability of the public school system—particularly in our big cities—to meet this challenge. While some critics are saying simply that our big city school systems are a failure, others are saying that they are outright pathological and should be destroyed if they cannot be reformed.

The Kerner Commission on Civil Disorders, for example, made the assertion that the educational system in the slums and ghettos has failed in its efforts to teach black youngsters. The commission backed this assertion with evidence that in the critical skills—verbal and reading ability—Negro students fall farther behind whites with each year of school completed. In the metropolitan Northeast, Negro students start school with slightly lower scores than whites on standard achievement tests; by sixth grade, Negroes are 1.6 grades behind; and by twelfth grade, 3.3 grades behind. By twelfth grade, many have left school. In the metropolitan areas of the North and West, a Negro student is more than three times as likely as a white to drop out of school by the time he is 17. The commission's typical participant in civil disorders was found to be a high school dropout.

In the recently publicized review of reforms, "One Year Later," by the Urban Coalition and Urban America, it was concluded that today "the indictment of failure passed on education in the slums and ghettos is just as valid and even more familiar."

The "One Year Later" report goes on to add this somber assessment:

Perhaps no measure of the break in faith with the public school system is as telling as the proposals coming from all sorts of respectable people— conservative economist Milton Friedman, Henry Levin of Stanford University, and Dean Theodore Sizer and Christopher Jencks of the Harvard Graduate School of Education—that parents of poor children be given public funds in the form of vouchers to "shop" for a better education in competing nonreligious private schools.

This radical (and possibly illegal) idea is supported by the success of the educational programs that have sprung up outside of the "straight" school system—the street academies, the MIND program, black culture storefront schools. Although these reach only a fraction of the youngsters rejected by the schools, they demonstrate the simple truth that the same student who fails in one situation can succeed in another.

In a report issued by the Department of Labor's Manpower Administration in 1968, the author said that on the basis of her evidence the public school dropouts or "pushouts" are simply

> ... youngsters who have reacted to inflexibility of some teachers and some school systems in holding the interest of the students, in developing their particular capabilities, and in dealing with them as individuals rather than as captive subjects. Often the reason for failing to complete high school is economic, or due to problems at home. In many situations where the school subject is not related to the real world or where the school situation could have been spiritually destructive, the dropout may have made the healthier choice than the passive student who simply endured.

Charles E. Silberman, author of the best-selling *Crisis in Black and White,* which had a profound influence on the early childhood and youth programs of the antipoverty effort, is now completing a 2½ year study of our public schools for the Carnegie Corporation. Silberman's tentative conclusions were reported in the *New York Times:*

> The public schools are quite literally destructive of human beings. They are the most grim and joyless places on the face of the earth. . . . What's wrong has much less to do with technique or substance than with the mindlessness of the whole enterprise. Nobody's encouraged to think about the purpose of his work, why he's doing what he does. What's wrong with schools is not that teachers don't know what they're teaching, but that they don't know why they're teaching it—what the relation of their subject is to the rest of knowledge as well as to life. No one is liberally educated unless he's forced to think about the nature of education. In large part this is what our student rebels are complaining about: this God-awful word "relevance."

While I think Silberman's assessment may be a little harsh, it does seem that he has hit on a key which may be most useful to those of us seeking to arouse in the disadvantaged a new interest in reading and learning. That key is *relevance.*

Issues that are relevant to today's students, particularly to the disadvantaged youth, must become a central concern of curriculum development and teacher participation. It would seem to me incumbent upon those responsible for the involvement of students at the elementary and secondary levels to strengthen their own awareness in four often-related areas:

- The existence of attending factors in the lives of students who are members of minority groups or who come from backgrounds of economic or social deprivation.
- Developments in the nation's economy which will influence occupational demand and which will increasingly call for an end to what former Assistant Secretary of Labor Stanley H. Ruttenberg has called "the artificial cleavage between vocational education and academic education."
- The growing number of government programs in manpower training, community services, and education which are designed to support and assist the severely deprived in their efforts to become productive participants in society.
- New tools, techniques, research, and other developments related to education and the reading process itself.

The public education system in this country today is probably in its gravest crisis since Horace Mann charted the course some 100 years ago. If it is to be saved (and I think it should be) then, probably, it can be done best by instructional supervisors and curriculum planners who have the wisdom and courage to join with those forces in the community who would make education responsive and responsible to the communities served.

Christopher Morley said, "There are three ingredients to the good life: learning, earning, and yearning." It is within our power to make this dream of the good life come true. To paraphrase McLuhan, reading is both the message and the medium.

Reactions to the Relevance of Reading

OTHO ROBINSON: We live in a world of language in which communication in every form—reading, speaking, viewing, listening—is the medium for learning, understanding, participating, contributing, and adapting. These skills are increasingly vital in many endeavors, and at various employment levels are essential to learning and earning a living. This latter requirement highlights the relevance and importance of reading.

More and more, the word *relevance* is used synonymously with *mean-*

ing. For a thing to have meaning, it has to involve the participation of the learner. Strong cases have been made for the relevance of reading. My concern is the large number of youngsters who may not be prepared to participate meaningfully in an increasingly competitive society; the psychological impact that this inability to compete has on the individual; and the economic, sociological, and political implications that this lack of preparedness may lead to an expanded welfare state.

A distinguishing characteristic of the institution of slavery was the master-servant-dependency relationship. In this respect, the possibilities of a welfare state represent a parallel form of slavery. If reading is the instrument through which learning and understanding emerge, if reading is an extremely important tool in one's earning a living, and if we are failing to equip youngsters with this important tool, we are in effect creating or adding to the development of a welfare state.

Now I ask Mann: What is the relationship between the technological revolution and this new environment? Is there a cause and effect relationship? Is this need and ability (or lack of ability) to communicate creating what is referred to as a "frightening collection of impressions?"

Is the emergence of so many terms and developments with their infinite meanings a form of adaptation or an attempt to adapt to a technological society—a society in which the individual may have hidden fears of his own ability to compete and may feel threatened? Is he experiencing a "copout?" Or does this "now" environment represent a crying out on the part of the student to educators and other adults so that, together, they can discover, plan, and seek out those experiences that will help youngsters become contributing members of society?

Is the student asking for a learning climate in which he talks and the teacher listens? Must we go beyond the classroom to find those experiences which have relevance? In this age of technocracy or technology, are the tools that appeal to sound- and sight-making experiences meaningful for the youngsters? It is not new for the student to participate in the planning of the program of instruction; textbook after textbook suggests the involvement of the student in this process. Perhaps we should involve the student to a greater degree.

MARION HENLEY: Today, everybody is talking about relevancy, and many people hate the very word. Most often, I found the reason to be that the word makes one feel uncomfortable.

When relevancy is used in connection with reading, one may become confused. Some of us agree that most inner-city students either cannot read, do not read, or have no incentive to read. We ask, "Why?" Who is going to be equal? Society determines who is going to be equal by whom it decides to educate. Such terms as *disadvantaged, slow learners, indigent, maximum feasible participation of the poor,* and *basic, essential,* and *regular students* demonstrate our dilemma and sometimes serve as tools to further dehumanize our students. *Social deprivation* is another term; and every time it is used I ask myself, "By whose values are we calling people socially deprived?"

When we talk about the inability of students to learn how to read, it is ironic that the educational system often victimizes the student by holding him responsible for his own failure. The question might be asked: Why should he learn to read? A child has nothing to do with the law that says he must go to school at the age of five!

It is suggested that the *poor, deprived* child must have a Head Start experience in order to be successful. (I am not speaking against Head Start when I make this point.) Some experts are going so far as to say that children from certain areas are hopeless from birth. Obviously, forces outside the child are responsible even though some people blame the child when he becomes a so-called dropout (actually a pushout).

According to Edwin C. Berry, in an article in the *Illinois Journal,* a gigantic Head Start program is needed for all the white middle- and upper-class decision makers in our society.

I once heard a man say that the role of formal education is to bring students in, get them ready, and then send them forth. Now, to me, this statement is a challenge. It does not state that we must accept one traditional route, nor does it say that we must do it between certain hours on certain days or during certain months. It does imply, however, that we must be creative in our responses to the challenge and that we must complete our jobs. This aim has not been reached and is not being reached for thousands of young people in the inner city.

I have often wondered about field trips. If you are in the same school for a year or two, you will discover that field trips are usually planned for the same location each year.

When a child, I went to Brookfield Zoo for eight years straight. Every time I went there I saw the same things. I used to think to myself, "When I grow up and have children, I will never force them to take a trip with the school to Brookfield Zoo." In the first place, too many children went at one time. Half of the time was spent just keeping up with everybody. And even as we grew up and the teachers would more fully prepare us for the trip, they never asked us, "What would you like to see when you get there?"

Once in eighth grade, I asked the teacher, "Why is it that we have to go and see the apes and the birds?"

And she said to me, "The route is set according to the way that the least number of children will be lost."

The experience, it was explained, would prepare me to learn something about animals. Had it not been for my mother and father, I probably never would have known about anything but apes and birds. Unfortunately, instead of broadening my world, what I enjoyed most from the trips was simply being away from school.

Some of my friends in education tell me things are different now. Yet even today when mass media have brought everything much closer to us and when TV is expanding the world of young people, still my fifth grade niece comes to report, "Guess where we are going? To the Brookfield Zoo."

Most of us, if we are honest, will acknowledge that textbooks are dull. And why are they dull? We are told it is because they must be technically correct. To be correct, textbooks must include black America's contributions, which have been systematically excluded in the past. The dullness of the reading material generally used is a part of what we are really talking about. The subject matter is rarely written in the student's life pattern. The world the school presents to the black student is not real to him, for it is not part of his daily life.

My observations are not new. I take hope in the fact that they are now coming out into the open. Mann has referred to isolated cases where new things are being tried. These cases are simply too few in number. Small groups all around our country are discussing this serious problem. Unfortunately, activity is limited to educators with little representation from the community served or from the student who may be victimized.

Hostilities may develop when community and students ask to be "in" on what is happening to them. A wave of fear about going into the unknown may result and a certain amount of fear may be expected. After a time one begins to wonder what it is that is really being feared. Is it the finding of solutions with which certain groups might not want to deal— such as hiring black textbook consultants, black writers, and black educators, not just for show but for what they know? In other words, don't just hire people; allow them to be consultants, writers, and educators.

I can remember classes in reading and I can remember uninteresting educational materials used. I can further remember the difficulty I had with them. I particularly want to add my concern to that of Mann with this often repeated statement, "reading must come before one can learn." Learning goes on daily, but I am afraid reading does not. I agree with Silberman that many of our teachers teach reading but often do not know why.

Our time is running out. We have thousands of youngsters tuning out, unable to operate in our world today. I would hope that it would become clear to us that we cannot teach reading in a vacuum. This is *now*, the time to learn how to read. We must find a way to challenge students to want to learn how to read. In order to do it I believe we have to look at the team approach. Educators have to realize that a lot of people are involved with the child. I believe that when the educators, the community, the student, and the parents themselves work together in a team, reading will no longer need to be stressed or distressing but will become an accepted part of education.

NORMAN BRADBURN: My first reaction, when this conference was announced was of surprise. I though the question of relevance of reading to social change was so self-evident that no need to confer existed. But, after some thought, I realized that we need to examine some underlying assumptions on which we operate, particularly those of us who work professionally in the field.

Many years ago I spent a year as a student in Turkey. In preparation for this visit, I learned some basic Turkish and a little bit about reading and speaking Turkish. After I had been in Istanbul a month, I was waiting for a streetcar one day when a resident came up to me and said, as the streetcar was approaching, "Where is this car going?" I was flattered, thinking I was passing for a native after only having been there for a month.

The same thing happened to me quite frequently, and I thought it was marvelous that people should think I knew my way around so well. Then I began to reflect. Why were people asking *me*? Why didn't they know themselves? So I asked a few Turkish friends, and it finally dawned on us what the problem was: the people couldn't read. As the streetcars came up the hill with their destinations plainly indicated, a number of the people waiting still didn't know the destination because they couldn't read.

This was my first experience in a culture where a very large proportion of the people absolutely could not read a word of their own language. What it began to bring home to me was how I, knowing relatively little of the language, could operate in a foreign environment because I was able to learn about it through reading. And I could increase my knowledge every day far more greatly than the people who were living there all the time.

The key to reading ability is the ability to increase knowledge at a fast rate, to learn *how* to read, and to be able to improve continuously. These are the important aspects of the kind of basic skills essential to reading.

Rutledge brought up an important point. In a way I think I would stress it even more than he did by alluding to some of the kinds of changes going on in society, changes which will affect not only the people who are in school at the moment but all of us who, if we are not already technologically obsolete, will be so in the not too distant future unless we continue to upgrade our skills. The basic tools of upgrading—reading, writing, and mathematics—are of first importance.

I looked around at some of the research my organization has been engaged in over the past ten years. One of the big studies done by one of my colleagues was a study of adult education and of how much of this kind of skills upgrading was going on among the adult population. In 1962 there were 5 million adults, or roughly one in five, engaged in some kind of formal educational activity beyond formal schooling; that is, they were engaged in kinds of adult education programs which met in more or less formal environments. Nine million of these efforts were job related and about three and a half million were in general education. So, about half of the people engaged in adult education were engaged in the kinds of educational programs related to improving either basic skills or their job related skills.

Along with this changing technology, its rapidity and its consequences, there is another interesting finding: the relationship between interest in and the pursuit of some sort of continuing education and one's occupational mobility and job improvement after entering the labor force.

Much of this discussion has focused on schools and helping people through the formal education system and into the labor force; a great deal of emphasis should also be given to what happens after joining the labor force—specifically, the ability to move up.

One of the findings in the study is the strong relationship between *occupational optimism* (the expectation that one's future occupational achievements will be better and that one hasn't reached the end of advancement) and interest in learning more and actively doing something about that interest. The relationship is stronger among older people and those people with less formal education.

If you lose your interest in continuing to upgrade your skills, you may find yourself very rapidly at a dead end in your own job. It may mean that under the best circumstances you just stay there; under less favorable circumstances, with the degree of change that is going on, it may mean that you find yourself unemployed at forty-five or fifty or out of the labor force—something which has happened to an increasing number of people. This is one aspect of the problem needing more emphasis.

Turning to some of the comments previously mentioned, I have some general reactions to share with you.

Why should learning to read be a problem at all? Learning to talk isn't a particular problem, so why should reading necessarily be a problem? Somehow, they seem very similar types of activities, certainly similar in their importance in regard to functioning in the world. Can we learn anything from some of the research about language acquisition which might be relevant in some way to some of the problems of learning to read?

There is the notion that there are certain periods in development when some kinds of skills can be learned more easily than at other times. There seems to be a kind of critical period for learning language, before which it is practically impossible for a child to learn to speak; during which language is rapidly and easily acquired; and after which it becomes extremely difficult, if not impossible, for one to acquire a certain skill. It seems likely that there may be critical periods for learning to read. Somewhere around five years to seven or eight is the critical period for learning to read; the period when a child can learn rapidly and rather easily.

The second thing about learning language—that is, learning to talk or speak—is that it is typically done in an informal setting where parents teach their children to talk with no great hoo-ha about it. Everybody does it; we may do it well or badly, but we all manage to convey it to our children.

Another thing is that much greater effort, or at least effort over a concentrated shorter period of time, goes into teaching a child to talk than goes into trying to teach a child to read. If we put as much effort into teaching a child to read as we put into teaching him to talk, might we get equivalent results?

A third thing about learning to speak is that speaking is extremely relevant to getting what one wants. It is a mutual benefit to both parent and child. The child learning to speak is highly motivated to learn to be able to communicate to make his wants known. It also becomes very important to the adult to get the child to learn to communicate. There is strong motivation on both sides. I think we would all agree that if you increase or make more obvious the relationship between reading and getting what one wants out of life, then reading would come more rapidly. The aspect of relevance is essentially a problem of motivation. Why should a child learn how to read if he can get what he wants without learning to read?

There are other things besides relevance that are important in learning to read. One is the psychological concept called negative transfer. When you learn math, essentially at the very beginning, you don't have anything to unlearn. There is no negative transfer from other kinds of experiences that you have had or that you have to unlearn before you can get on with math. There are some problems of negative transfer in learning how to read. One is the problem of the relationship between the materials that are read and the student's vocabulary or language structure, syntax, and mode of speech.

If there are essentially two modes of speech, there are two modes of communication—speech patterns and written words. The written words differ in a really significant way from the way in which people speak. There would be certain negative transfer problems, if the reading task is seen as converting what we do verbally into some sort of written symbols. If you are trying to make a one-to-one correspondence—that is, with people speaking entirely differently from the way the materials they are reading are written—

then you are going to have a negative transfer. People are going to have to unlearn some material before they can get on with reading.

The final point I want to share is that people learn to read in spite of what we do rather than because of what we do. Somehow or other, learning to read can't be that difficult since most people do it in spite of all the things that we throw in their way. Sometimes discussions about the techniques of teaching reading get much more complicated than they should be. How to translate techniques into positive action may be difficult. It is possible that certain organizational necessities get in the way of accomplishment. There is, for example, an assumption in all systems—public, private, and from elementary to college level—that standards are terribly important. (By this, I mean that people should read or learn certain kinds of things but not other kinds of things.) Perhaps we have overemphasized the surplus meaning, the content, of the material that is used to teach a skill, for we can get hung up on relevancy as well. Much of the criticism directed towards existing materials has been that they are irrelevant, meaning that the people who have been writing or adapting these materials have been so concerned about the content that the result has been some very vapid, value-free, and, unfortunately, interest-free material which barely manages to get the skills across. I think we worry too much about it; I think we have worried too much about keeping controversial material out.

Second is the importance that all systems place on maintaining the image of expertness of the teacher. This trait is especially true of colleges. Teachers in one aspect or another are defined as experts, but too much energy is used trying to defend or protect our standing as experts who inevitably know what is right and wrong. This is in direct contradiction to the research which suggests, that for a lot of areas in learning there is no right or wrong way. In fact, lots of different ways work; in some instances, none work.

The third thing which has to be faced is that there are some very real economic problems, such as the money some schools have invested in reading materials. There is often resistance to change of materials because of cost, cost not only in the strict sense of how much has been invested in textbooks or teaching aids but also a kind of psychological cost on the part of teachers who are using the materials. If you change materials, you have to reorient and invest more of yourself. Many teachers may not be willing to adapt.

Finally, there is a need to use other kinds of personnel. I would argue that learning to read need not involve only experts. I think that fourth and fifth graders can learn something by helping first graders.

JAMES W. MANN: I would like to respond to Robinson's question about the cop out which is central. The child who cops out is one who does it because of social pressures he can neither understand nor deal with. I think in many instances it is a matter of fear, confusion, lack of confidence, insecurity, and sometimes downright hurt.

In developing a tentative theory about children in these situations, we find that, depending on the nature of the child psychologically, children under pressure tend either to move toward withdrawal as a means of preservation or survival or they move toward aggression as the opposite method of survival and of dealing with situations. This reaction is what we are seeing. The school can moderate either extreme of behavior to some extent simply by freeing the situation and being less demanding of things that don't really count or don't count very much at this time by offering some kind of activity which gives the child a chance to get a feeling of worth.

The danger here is simply stopping with adjustment; adjustment is not enough. It isn't enough just to make the children more comfortable. We have to help them find a visible bridge to the outside world.

Women's Talent Corps / College
for Human Services

Audrey C. Cohen

THE WOMEN'S TALENT CORPS (WTC) was founded in 1964 and incorporated in March 1965 at a time when civil rights, militancy, and the demand for integrated quality education had reached new heights. Against this background, two related problems came into sharp focus in the minds of the WTC founders: the need to "humanize" and expand services in the social sector of the economy and the need to utilize the talent and energy of people living in disadvantaged areas who were unemployed or underemployed.

The revolution that is challenging the stability of society is concerned with a fundamental change in manpower usage on the one hand and the rising expectations of minorities on the other.

The major areas for absorbing manpower in the future will be in the service sector—health, education, social services, crime prevention, narcotics prevention, and a whole range of publicly supported services. It is predicted that education and health together may employ 25 or 35 percent of the entire labor force before another generation passes.

If we look at these areas today, we find that a serious shortage of professional personnel already exists. As a result, central city urban schools are failing to provide a decent quality of literacy and education to most minority group children. The systems of health, welfare, and justice are in equally poor condition.

As American society becomes increasingly a white collar economy, what hope is there for the low-income, inner-city resident, handicapped immediately by an inadequate education? How are we to improve the human services? Where are we to find the professional personnel to fill the existing agencies, let alone the additional ones required by a service-oriented society?

Our new professionals must come from the largest untapped source of manpower that we now have—our poor—*and they must know how to read.* But there must also exist the opportunity for them to use their education! What is the point of educating a population only to slam shut the doors, supposedly opened to them by that education, because of race?

Funded by the Office of Economic Opportunity in 1966 under a Title 207 demonstration grant, the Talent Corps sought to solve this dilemma. It proposed to 1) train citizens from low-income areas to serve as paraprofessionals in the overburdened, understaffed community service agencies of New York City and 2) create permanent jobs in these agencies where none had previously existed by demonstrating in practice what trained community people could do. It was also hoped that bringing community residents into schools, hospitals, and settlement houses would help reduce the growing distrust and even hostility between professionals in social service and the community they served.

The College for Human Services is a natural extension of the original New Careers training program of the WTC. Talent Corps graduates, seeking additional education which would enable them to rise in a career toward professional status, found the traditional colleges closed to them or irrelevant.

At the College for Human Services we are developing alternate routes to the professions. Our students are provided with both academic and practical training and are judged on their performance in both areas. As the effectiveness of the work-study approach becomes apparent, its use for professional education is increasing.

How are we able to overcome the deficiencies and problems in which the schools originally failed? The College for Human Services not only works to overcome educational deficiencies and remedy basic skills but simultaneously plunges the student into a mature and useful learning program. The student sees immediately that he will have a position to enter as a pre-professional and, once having broken through the barriers, a chance to continue developing a career.

Let us consider one student, Dolores G., for an illustration of one solution to the problems of manpower usage, rising expectations, and literacy. Mrs. G. arrived from Puerto Rico (where she was born) when she was about 14. She had had a difficult childhood and was left very much to her own devices once she came to New York City. Mrs. G. did manage to get her high school diploma by attending evening sessions, but her attempts to find advanced job training (for example, in x-ray technology) were unsuccessful. She soon married and had children; but marital difficulties arose, and her unhappiness and insecurity led her to cut herself off from the outside world and turn more and more inward.

When Mrs. G.'s children entered school, her interest and concern for their education and other children, in general, led a community worker to notice her and suggest she might be interested in applying to the Talent Corps for the kind of training which would enable her to put her natural talents and skills to use.

Mrs. G. was accepted by the Talent Corps, whose entrance requirements were simply that she be over 21, that she meet the federal criteria for low income (she was on welfare at the time), that she be able to read and write, and that she exhibit a commitment to improving her community. The placement test she was given subsequent to her acceptance (the ABLE II) showed only sixth grade ability in the basic skills, despite her high school diploma. Mrs. G.'s behavior mirrored her weaknesses—she was shy, hesitant, and self-conscious about participating in class discussions, despite the seminar format of small informal groups.

How do you go about reaching a person like this? Could the traditional institutions of higher education have helped a woman like Mrs. G.? In view of the level of her basic skills would she have been accepted there? What would she have learned there that would have filled her needs? Why do we need an institution like the College for Human Services in the first place?

If we are going to develop a society where man is more important than his technology, our colleges and universities are going to have to begin to dedicate themselves to services rather than education for its own sake; and this direction in turn implies the introduction of a radical new curriculum, a change in credentialing patterns, and new institutions that can respond to this challenge. The middle-class students' cry for relevance is only one symptom of how important such innovation has become to society.

We, too, were so used to thinking about standard curricula that it was a year before we attempted to remove the disciplinary walls that bind our minds and before we conceived of a curriculum that truly integrates and interweaves the elements of the helping professions in a new way.

In certain respects the challenge facing the Talent Corps/College for Human Services in developing its curriculum is similar to that facing liberal arts colleges today. Both are asking how to keep human values at the forefront of education in an age when so many people consider professional training more important than individual growth and development as educational goals. Colleges no longer prepare students for life in a society of men, according to Archibald MacLeish, but for employment in a specialized profession or industry. In fact, says another critic of today's educational philosophy, the idea of a liberal education is disappearing altogether.

The entire conception of a liberal education—of the most serious ideas of our civilization being taught by professors who took them seriously—has disappeared under pressure of one kind or another. . . . I believe that, when students demand that their studies be relevant, this is what they are unwittingly demanding. After all, what could be more "relevant" today than the idea of "political obligation"—philosophy—or the meaning of "justice"? And, in fact, on the few campuses where such teaching still exists, the students do find it "relevant" and exciting and illuminating.*

Given this broader interpretation of human service, what kind of curriculum will best prepare students to work in the field of human services? Clearly, it cannot be a curriculum devoted solely to professional techniques and remedial skills, important as these are as elements of the total program. It must attempt in some way to provide a new perspective on man himself, his nature, his purposes in life, and his value system. It must create a consciousness of values and of the value choices made by human beings. It must talk about the kind of society we have and the kind we want. It must talk, finally, about ways of changing society so that its institutions will reflect human needs.

The core curriculum developed by the College for Human Services attempts to do just that. Its approach is interdisciplinary, lifting useful concepts from their usual narrow contexts and applying them to practical human situations facing students on the job. Students bring back problems from the field for further discussion and to explore how the theories affect the practice. There is constant interplay between classroom and field.

Students spend two days a week at the college and three days a week in the field. While they work in the agencies, students are supervised both by the professional under whom they function and the faculty member assigned to that particular placement. The faculty's function in the field is both to provide feedback to insure that the curriculum remains receptive to the needs of the students and to perform as liaison between agency, Talent Corps, and student.

Mrs. G. participated in all core curriculum seminars, research projects, remedial sessions, and field work. She was particularly successful in her placement as an educational assistant in a school in the Bronx, where her knowledge of Spanish and her ability to relate to the children were especially important.

The development of communication skills and the correction of educational deficiencies took place concurrently with field experience and the presentation of concepts. For Mrs. G. daily practice was required, followed by immediate, friendly criticism. Almost any piece of written work might be considered fair game for critical analysis: weekly activity reports, student

* Kristol, Irving. "A Different Way to Restructure the University," *New York Times Magazine*, December 8, 1968.

logs, special themes, book reports, reviews of newspaper articles or TV programs, and written comments on lectures.

"I corrected errors, commented on the content, and asked for a rewrite of unclear paragraphs," explained a Talent Corps faculty member in describing how she helped students improve their basic skills. "I supplemented vocabulary lists by adding nuisance words culled from the students' own written exercises. I analyzed these words for their meanings, nuances, and the word roots. I read aloud from book reports and invited discussion."

Another technique was to relate remedial work to the substance of learning related to human services. A speech by a hospital director, for example, provided the basis for a sentence-correction assignment which included such sentences as the following:

- "Social work (have, has) both rehabilitative and preventive aspects."
- "Some (patients, patience) seek out the social worker directly."
- "In addition to (sitting, setting) the standards for medical care, the medical board also (determines, determine) the qualifications for attending physicians."

Two groups of students were given special attention. The group which tested lower on diagnostic tests attended special tutorial sessions developed by a faculty member specializing in remedial work. Five volunteer tutors plus two Urban Corps workers provided the kind of one-to-one relationship which Mrs. G. and other students needed in order to learn rapidly. Marked improvement resulted from this saturation effort. The group which tested higher was also given special attention. Those showing achievement above the eighth grade level in either English or mathematics were invited to participate in special classes.

The satisfaction of her successful experience in the field gave Mrs. G. the impetus to apply herself increasingly to the academic work in the program and even to solving some of her personal problems. She became interested in outside activities and began to attend regularly community meetings about schools and the role of the paraprofessional.

The new-found strength and interest stimulated in Mrs. G. by her work in the Talent Corps was reinforced and reflected in her reading. Post-testing placed her reading at almost ninth grade level—a gain of almost three years in thirty weeks. Her principal has written that if she were to continue with her studies, she would be an outstanding teacher in the school system. She has requested that the College for Human Services accept her back for the sophomore year.

Why is it that Mrs. G. and other students were successful in their search for education and training this time? What were the factors which contributed to their lack of success on other attempts?

We at the Talent Corps are convinced that for many others like our students there was the pervasive feeling that no one really cared what happened to them; that they, as individuals, were unimportant; that their talents, experience, and ideas counted for nothing. Within their own families, as well as in their larger communities, there was no evidence that the education they were expected to complete would lead to a job, let alone security of any kind.

At the Talent Corps, for the first time in their lives, they are met with the expectation on the part of someone else that they can succeed. They are encouraged at every step by someone working with them to assure their success and offer help and encouragement during the difficult moments. Shortly after she began her training, Mrs. G. wrote in her autobiography: "Joining the Women's Talent Corps is something unexpected. Every day with you is another door open to the light."

Another contributing factor is the instant feedback from what the students are doing. Errors are tackled immediately, and correction and learning take place quickly. The students are given responsibility for part of their progress by using programed materials which work on the principle of success at each step.

Most important, perhaps, is the use, in the remedial program, of material relevant to the interests of our students. The development of such materials has required Herculean effort on the part of our staff, since they have had to find readings both interesting to adult students and meaningful to the study of the human services. The conceptual level we seek coordinates with the information and theories the students are discussing in their course work.

For students whose motivation is high to begin with, the stimulus of grasping the abstract concepts and of being introduced to new theories, ideas, and new ways of approaching life and its situations is, in many cases, all that is needed to "open the door to light."

There is no question that the improvement in the literacy level of our students has an important bearing on their ability to undertake and perform at a job. Aside from the practical skills acquired, they can now read, comprehend, and apply theories and concepts of the related academic fields. They are looked upon by their professional supervisors as much more than just helpful community aides. They begin to see themselves as capable of attaining professional status and thus able to improve the human services of their communities. In sum, their new skills and resulting self-image make these people the vital key to the resurrection of the community.

Reading Improvement Programs
in General Motors

Harry O. Patterson

GENERAL MOTORS CORPORATION has had one of the longest continuous reading improvement programs in industry. Starting in 1952, Dan Jones, a senior instructor at General Motors Institute, began an extensive program of research in this area. The objective of this study was to determine ". . . the most practical methods of improving the reading efficiency of members of the various levels of management" (2). At that time most of the research in adult reading had used college students. Not much had been done concerning adult reading training. For some time, General Motors had been concerned with the reading efficiency of its management personnel because of the increasing amount of reading necessary to carry out the various functions of the corporation.

In early 1952 GMI, in cooperation with the AC Spark Plug Division, began developing a training program to increase the reading efficiency of top management personnel. In a short time several of the divisions of the corporation became interested in the program.

GMI is the central educational facility of GMC. As such, it consists of the five-year cooperative Engineering Program leading to a bachelor's degree in mechanical, industrial, and electrical engineering, and now a bachelor's degree in industrial administration, also on the cooperative basis; the Continuing Engineering and Part Time Education Department; and the Management Training Department. It was with the cooperation of this latter department that the early development of the program was inaugurated.

After an extensive preliminary study of existing programs—both academic and industrial—a review of research, and discussions with authorities in the field, recommendations were presented to a committee of corporation personnel who were to act as an advisory group. Jones' major recommendation was that the program should be started on an experimental basis because of the conflicting theories concerning training. By making use of an experimental approach, it would be possible to evaluate the effectiveness of various methods of training. Other recommendations were to treat reading problems on an individual basis and for a follow-up evaluation some months after training.

With the acceptance of specific program designs by the committee, the development and assembly of practice reading materials that would interest industrial executives began. These materials included exercises to improve eye movements, reading rate, vocabulary, evaluative reading, and degree of comprehension. These were later developed into a manual for use by GMC. The educational editions of the *Reader's Digest* and the *Atlantic Monthly* were used as supplementary materials. In addition to these, each participant in the program was asked to bring personal reading material of his own choosing, such as novels, hobby books, magazines, and material from his job. Reading accelerators, a group tachistoscope, and reading films were used under controlled conditions.

After the development of sufficient materials, a pilot training program composed of GMI faculty was formed, enabling this program to be debugged and additional material to be developed. Several experimental groups were then formed at the AC Spark Plug Division. This study was made to determine, under controlled conditions, which of several methods of training was most effective. Approximately one-half of the participants were engineers, and the average improvement in reading ability was about one hundred-ten percent. It was also found, through this study, that training could be as effective without machines as with machines and that positive results were retained over an extended period. More will be said of this aspect later in this paper.

Following the AC Spark Plug Division program, other programs were conducted on a research basis with other divisions, central office staff personnel, and GMI engineering students. The program offered to the engineering students was modified to fit into the school section of their cooperative education and to minister to the specific needs of students in terms of textbook reading and study habits.

Since the inception of the General Motors Reading Improvement Program, there have been a number of variations devised to accommodate the different groups involved in the program. Some of these have already been briefly mentioned. Following is more detail of each one.

Following the initial programs at AC Spark Plug Division and at other locations in the corporation, the two members of the faculty who with Jones were instrumental in developing the program were kept busy traveling to the various units to give the program to management personnel. It was soon realized that a different approach was necessary since each of the faculty members had teaching responsibilities in the cooperative phase of the engineering program. To circumvent this problem, a one-week training program was developed to teach members of the Management Training Department, selected on the basis of their having a background in psychology, the techniques, philosophy, and skills necessary to present the program. This kind of background was believed to be the most appropriate for an understanding of the Reading Improvement Program. Since 1963, however, the Management Training Department has trained its own personnel. It is estimated that between 1959 and the present approximately twenty-five persons were trained to conduct the program.

The original program was designed to be of twenty-four hours' duration, spread over a twelve-week period. In some instances, this timing was not possible; the reading improvement techniques therefore, were incorporated into a communications skills program offered as a forty-hour resident program at GMI. In this program, personnel from several divisions meet for skill development in speaking, writing, listening, and reading. It is offered two-to-four times a year, and each session is attended by ten-to-twelve men.

Other attempts have been made from time to time to make reading improvement a part of other programs. These, however, have met with limited success for several reasons. The General Motors Overseas Operation Sales Program is one such effort. This is a six-week resident program for sales personnel from General Motors units around the world. The reading improvement part of the program was eliminated after three years because of the difficulty with the English language encountered by some of the participants from non-English speaking countries. The major reason for eliminating it from other programs was that a higher priority was placed on other subjects.

Since 1964, three hundred thirty-two managers have participated in the General Motors Reading Improvement Program on an in-plant basis. It might be of interest to note the various parts of the corporation from which these persons came.

It will also be noted that most of the participants are from the overseas division—in the New York office—and the operations, financial, and legal staffs. These are segments of the corporation in which a great amount of paper work is done in contrast to the operating divisions which are primarily concerned with manufacturing.

	CAR DIVISIONS	BODY & ASSBLY	AUTO. COMP	DAYTON, HSHOLD APPL. & ELECTRO	OVER-SEAS	OPERATIONS, FINANCIAL & LEGAL STAFFS
1964	23	0	28	0	75	11
1965	12	0	18	0	15	25
1966	2	1	13	0	26	0
1967	0	0	0	0	24	18
1968	0	0	0	0	22	19

The reading improvement program is one among a host of other training programs that are being conducted for all levels of management in GMC throughout the year. In 1968, for example, over 17,000 managers of all levels participated in the training programs offered by the Management Training Department.

PART TIME PROGRAM

The Part Time Program is, in effect, an adult continuing education program for industry made available to all who live within commuting distance of GMI. Because of the large number of General Motors plants in this area, most of the enrollees are employees of GM, although there are a number of noncorporation persons also participating.There are actually three groups of courses in this activity: management, executive and professional development, and special. These are nondegree courses in which no college credit is given. The courses are given on a tuition refund basis for GM employees, provided a passing grade is received. The Part Time Program varies considerably from that given by the Management Training Department since most of the participants of the Part Time Program are not in the management group and do not have a college education, although most are high school graduates.

Those persons enrolled in the Management Program receive a certificate of completion upon the fulfillment of a required number of courses. The courses are offered during the day and evening since many of the enrollees work either the first or second shifts. The participants are primarily hourly employees who wish to prepare themselves for possible management positions or, if already in management, for advanced positions. All courses are of 12 weeks' duration.

Since 1963, there have been between 200 and 300 new enrollees. The reading improvement course scheduled in this program was mandatory for 85 to 90 percent of this number. On the basis of scores on a standardized reading test it is mandatory that those persons who score below a given level enroll in a remedial reading course provided by the Mott Foundation. For those who score above a given level the reading improvement course is waived. About 3 percent fall in the first category and 7 percent, in the second. The course, as it is now designed, is not remedial in nature and cannot be remedial under present circumstances. The Mott Foundation Reading Program is a remedial program and is equipped and staffed for such a purpose. Even though they qualify on the tests, there are a few in the Part Time Program who should, for their own benefit, be in a remedial program. These persons are given as much individual help and encouragement as possible without making them conspicuous in the group.

The size of each group in the Management Program is limited to sixteen. Because of shift changes and/or overtime work, members of each group change frequently. This condition does not seem to create too great a problem for the participants in that each instructor makes use of the same material. The Diagnostic Reading Test—Survey Section—is administered two or three times during the twelve weeks so that each person can observe his own progress. Each member also keeps an individual progress chart on which he indicates his rate, comprehension, and index for each selection read. Approximately one-fourth to one-third of the course is spent on pacers.

Prior to admittance into the Management Program each participant must show proficiency in English and basic mathematics as well as in reading— unless college credit courses have been completed. Enrollment in the Management Program is not recommended if test results in any one of the three areas is low. Typical of the courses offered in the Management Program are those in understanding human behavior, understanding business, American economic system, principles of supervision, principles of methods analysis, and basic financial concepts. Thus, it may be readily seen that proficiency in reading is a prerequisite to the successful completion of the program.

The Executive and Professional Development courses were developed to meet the specific needs of the manager, engineer, and college graduate who is familiar with the technical areas in which he works but feels the need for expanding his understanding in a chosen field. These courses are not offered in an established sequence but, as indicated, are selected by the participants on the basis of their needs. While the reading improvement course is not included in those offered at the present time, it is possible for an enrollee to take reading improvement. If a significant number of enrollees express an interest in reading improvement, it will be necessary to provide a more advanced course for them.

THE ENGINEERING AND INDUSTRIAL ADMINISTRATION PROGRAM

The curriculum of the Engineering and Industrial Administration Program is difficult, and the course load is high with each undergraduate student carrying approximately 24 credit hours with 28 to 31 contact hours a week, a schedule not leaving much time for additional course work even though reading skills are inadequate.

From 1954 through 1956, however, 367 students enrolled in the voluntary Reading Improvement Program. All levels of students from the second-semester freshmen through second-semester seniors were allowed to take the program. First-semester freshmen were not permitted in the program because it was believed that these students had enough difficulty adjusting to the college environment without adding an additional two-hour class to their schedules, even though voluntary.

Since 1957 a number of different approaches have been tried with limited success. One such approach was to limit enrollment in the program to first-semester sophomores. Another approach was to limit the program to those students who were having difficulty in their prescribed courses. These students were recommended to the Reading Improvement Program by their plant coordinators and their faculty advisors. It was quickly discovered that many of these students did not believe they had a reading problem and came into the program resenting the extra hours it required. At the same time, there was an expansion in the number of courses offered in the Department of Humanities and Social Science for which the staff for the Reading Improvement Program was needed. It was necessary, therefore, to cut back on the number of classes scheduled for reading improvement. Other problems began to appear. The program is listed in the catalog; and a number of students, other than those for whom it is recommended, request help each semester. Since it is difficult to get students with the same free hours in which to schedule organized classes, the present practice is to work with these students individually as much as possible. Because they do not use the reading laboratory on a scheduled basis, counseling with these students has not been especially successful.

The curriculum for students entering in Fall 1969 was reduced to 20 credit hours and no more than five subjects each semester. It was hoped that with this reduction in the class load, faculty time would again be available and more students would be able to enroll in the Reading Improvement program. Should this hope become a reality, the program would be augmented to consist of both reading and study skills improvement, with approximately five weeks being devoted to each area.

On an experimental basis, a study skills program is presently being conducted for freshmen who are having difficulty in physics, chemistry, and calculus. These students meet one evening a week for one hour over a four-week period. Study techniques for each of these courses, as well as general study techniques and listening skills are discussed. Reading efficiency is mentioned in these sessions, but no practice time is available. This program is too new to know what success has been achieved.

Industrial reading improvement programs, like many other training programs, are affected by economic conditions, fads, and organizational needs. In a recent survey of the top 500 corporations listed in *Fortune*, Allen Berger received responses from only 54. Many of the responding corporations said they refer employees to commercial reading firms or college and university programs rather than try to staff this kind of program (*1*). The response to the survey does not necessarily mean that those corporations that failed to answer feel that reading efficiency is unimportant. It could mean that their needs are many and complex and training must be conducted in areas other than reading. In many cases, a hierarchy of organizational training needs is established, and the place of reading training in this hierarchy varies a great deal. It can also mean that training in large or widely dispersed corporations is delegated to the training directors in the individual units. In this case, the corporate training director may not be aware of all of the training that is going on in these units as the author found to be the case in the responses received to questionnaires sent to representative corporations in a number of industries in 1956, 1958, and 1962 (*3*).

It is hoped that the present emphasis placed on speed reading will diminish and that more realistic approaches will be taken to increase the reading efficiency of employees at all levels of industry. For some employees, remedial programs are a necessity, but these are and will have to be conducted by reading specialists outside the organization.

I am confident that reading programs are and will continue to be a part of industrial training and that their use will be stimulated by the continuing growth of technology and the resulting reading demands placed on the individual.

REFERENCES

1. Berger, Allen, and Kathleen Olson. "Current Practices in Commercial, Corporate, and College and University Programs Designed to Increase Reading Efficiency," unpublished article.
2. Jones, Dan H. Reading Improvement in Industry Aided by a Scientific Program, *General Motors Engineering Journal*, 2 (1955), 22-25.
3. Patterson, Harry O. "Current Trends in Reading Improvement Programs in Industry," *New Developments in Programs and Procedures for College-Adult Reading*, Twelfth Yearbook of the National Reading Conference, 1962, 9-12.

Reading: A Case Study

Robert D. Johnson

NEW TO THE HISTORY of big business is commitment to education. While the function of a manufacturing company like Westinghouse is not primarily educational, more than ever industries are coming to realize a social responsibility in making available scientific findings, new ideas, and techniques that promise enrichment.

The implications this development suggests are boundless. Imagine the tremendous resources and the proven effectiveness of American industry being brought to bear on the problems of education. Picture the effects, in human terms, of the energy thus spent. And the possible returns for this investment, the mutual profits for this new alliance, stagger the imagination. It is the glorious partnership of Horace Mann and Andrew Carnegie.

Westinghouse Learning Corporation, a subsidiary of Westinghouse Electric, has accepted the challenge and the promise. This horizon–expanding involvement by a leader in production for the home, industry, and science reflects an evolving awareness that it is people, after all, who are our most important products.

The discussion here will concentrate on one small adventure in the fascinating expedition of Westinghouse Learning Corporation into the operation of a Job Corps Center.

The resident trainees are 16 to 21 years old, school dropouts or putouts, who have experienced failure in finding or keeping satisfactory work. They generally will fit into one or more of several categories: those with negative attitudes and/or offensive personalities and those who are underachievers or frustrated overachievers. Very simply, they lack the social or educational skills needed to get a job, function on the job, and get along with their fellowman.

Westinghouse, in the Job Corps Program, is not concerned with the vast majority of public school students who lead normal emotional, social, and academic lives: those who experience success in their school careers, marriages, jobs, and communities. On the contrary, Westinghouse Learning Corporation has picked up the challenge of taking over where public education has failed: with that 30 percent who have been tagged with epitaphs like *incorrigible, dropout, delinquent, misfit,* and worse. The experience has vividly demonstrated that such individuals can and do have a valuable contribution to offer if provided the opportunity.

To attack the question "Why do kids drop out of school?" would serve only to deepen the well-worn rut so many have trod. The education market is glutted with definitive studies of the deprived, the slow learner, and the culturally disadvantaged, *ad infinitum.* The probing instruments of research have laid bare the cancer in public education; the diagnosis is clear. Yet the problem of treatment remains. And that problem, the problem of salvaging the 800,000 young men and women who are each year thrown into humanity's scrap heap, is the real crisis in education.

It is to this challenge that Westinghouse Learning Corporation's Atterbury Job Corps Center addresses itself. Although the solutions this effort provides are not final and do not pull out the roots of the weed that so shamefully wastes human resources, they represent an impressive, and certainly relevant, frontal attack on the problem.

Atterbury is primarily a vocational training center. The emphasis is on job training. More and more though, the notion that vocational proficiency alone plays but a small role in the competitive theater of job-getting and job-keeping asserts its strength.

The real cause of failure, indicated by Job Corps records, is hauntingly echoed in the shopworn phrase "unacceptable behavior." Comments commonly seen are "refuses to accept responsibility"; "never shows up after payday"; "consistently late"; "poor attitude"; "couldn't get along." Rarely are these young men turned out because of poor qualifications.

It would seem, then, that the key to success is in altering behavior that is objectionable to industry and society. But trying to remold a young person with 18 years' previous conditioning in one to two years is a monumental assignment. It is not, however, altogether impossible.

Atterbury's successful operation is founded on the premise that marked behavior improvement *can* be effected: that it can be helped to come about through meaningfully sharing the experiences and the thoughts of others via reading and in the improved self-image that comes with satisfactory reading experience.

An outstanding example of the effects of this philosophy is the case of

David, who enrolled in September 1966. Though David's Job Corps career was extraordinarily successful, it represents the spirit of things at Atterbury.

David's behavior, as is all behavior, was learned. Surely a sizable contribution to his wealth of negative attitudes may be attributed to what has been called the "cumulative deficit phenomenon of the public school syndrome." At its best, this is the process of passing students on to succeeding grade levels because they come to school. At its worst—and it seems too often to be at its worst—it is the school's rejection of the individual, of his problems, his unique personality, his learning pace, his interests, tastes, and behavior.

It is the grand irony of universal education in a democracy that affirmations of individual worth on the one hand must be confronted with denial of that precept on the other. It is bold hypocrisy for the schools to hide behind a mask of benevolence, offering false and meaningless "success," while punishing nearly a third of their charges with course work that forces and reinforces failure.

The malignancy had worked with effective devastation on David. A handsome, well-developed New York black, he had completed eight troubled months of tenth grade when he was finally expelled from the public school in May 1966.

David was far behind his classmates in school work and possessed a truly fascinating record of school and legal offenses. He had registered no felonies, however, and was enrolled in the Job Corps by his probation officer as merely a "youthful offender."

Sixty-two enrollees stepped off the bus with David at the old bachelor officer's quarters Atterbury uses for housing the young men during their week-long orientation program. Adjustment to the highly structured routine at Atterbury is seldom an easy matter for new enrollees; and David, demonstrating an active intelligence and verbal facility, contributed abundantly to the rankled discourse that always accompanies the transition. The food was rotten; the beds were too hard. All the testing gave him headaches. The dormitory staff compiled a list of observations on his behavior, including such comments as "refused to make his bed and clean up his area"; "refused to get out of bed"; "insubordination"; and "threatening a resident counselor."

Because of his poor attitude, David's case was brought before the screening committee. They would decide if he would be allowed to remain in the program. In advance of the conference, however, the committee undertook to gather more background material on David in order to better understand the nature of his case and thereby facilitate the rendering of an equitable decision.

The following was accumulated from the records of his counselors and probation officer. At home, David and a younger sister lived with their parents. His stepfather, a car salesman, was away from home most of the time, and his mother, working varied shifts, frequently left the children home alone, responsible for their own discipline. By the time David had reached his twelfth year, he had spent much time on the streets. He and his family lived on the fourth floor of a large eight-floor tenement on the fringe of the ghetto district.

In school, David appeared to be a loner. He did not attend the same school as his neighborhood peers. After school, he chose activities with the gang, rather than sports. He often exhibited frustration with work in the large classes. One teacher wrote of him that he was a "lazy, impudent, dirty boy" who "could do better but just didn't care." He would not do his homework or participate in class. He had moved to New York from Miami when he was eight and was evaluated by his Miami grade school teacher as an apt student.

His eighth grade English teacher has reported that "his parents don't care." In the tenth grade during the last months of his school experience, David was truant two or three days every week. His discharge finally came about as the result of threats he had made to his male physical education teacher.

Out of school, David was a member of a small gang who called themselves The Disciples and was thought of as a leader in the group. He had been apprehended by the police several times on charges of curfew violation. Once he confessed to having experimented with drugs but added that he did not really like them. He had been placed on probation for shoplifting.

The results of the Stanford Achievement Test he had taken in orientation were called for, showing the following grade level scores:

Reading
Word Meaning	2.7
Paragraph Meaning	2.9
Language	3.2
Social Studies	3.8
Average	3.2

Math
Arithmetic Concepts	4.3
Arithmetic Computations	3.6
Arithmetic Application	4.9
Average	4.3

GATB Test Score: (General Aptitude Test Battery)
General Learning	74
Verbal Aptitude	76

David was scheduled for intensive counseling. His counselor submitted a recommendation that he be allowed to remain in the program and submitted his case study along with several suggested activities, promising to be beneficial to David and including a concentrated dose of individual instruction in reading. The screening committee concurred in the opinion that since a major cause of David's fraustration seemed to be his inability to experience important success situations, he could be placed in the reading program at a level where this need would be fulfilled. Hopefully, these success-oriented activities would begin to mold in David's mind a more acceptable image of himself and be reflected in the emergence of positive new behavior patterns. And, he would finally be learning to read. David was allowed to stay.

On the basis of his low reading ability, David was assigned to the prevocational program. This is an all-day activity aimed primarily at improving competency. With only nine classmates, it was possible for David to get all the individual attention he needed. At this time he was not scheduled for vocational training since most of the shop areas require a good deal of reading. It hardly seemed reasonable to continue pushing David at his frustration level and expect behavioral changes.

Those first sessions with David were very stormy ones. He was no fool. He had learned through the grapevine that he had been placed in one of the "dumb" classes. To say that he was hostile or belligerent would grossly understate the situation.

Fortunately for David, he had a model teacher. Dialogue was kept open and honest as David's instructor tried to communicate, calmly and respectfully, the reality and the importance of these first steps. He would not repeat many of the crimes already committed against David.

At this beginning level, David was not diagnosed to determine his place in the program; it was the program that was diagnosed to fit David. In order to ensure success, David's first activities had to be made both meaningful to him and at a level of difficulty in which he could operate effectively. The simultaneous accomplishment of these two criteria seemed impossible.

It was, therefore, decided to attack them one at a time, meaningful activity first, in order to motivate him. The instructor gave David a great deal of extra personal attention. David was allowed to answer the phone, lead in cleanup, and perform other routine chores. And he had an attentive listener when he just needed to talk. To this acceptance, David did respond. He was less often turbulent and became eager to accept new responsibilities.

By this time his teacher had reasonably well determined which of David's basic needs were being fulfilled and which would yet have to be met in order to get a total commitment from him. David's most important need, his instructor concluded, was to feel secure, second, to achieve. A conscious attempt was made to develop a pattern of response that would consistently feed and reinforce those needs. There was not an answer in class that David didn't get at least partly right, not a chore that he couldn't do, and not a bit of good behavior that went unnoticed.

David's teacher was convinced that a measure of David's overt behavior and impulsive tendencies were related to his short attention span, consequently, he adjusted David's schedule accordingly, shifting often to new activities. Intuitively, the teacher felt that the more serious behavioral problems came from boys who were generally "intelligent" and who knew they were underachievers or academically deficient. Without condescension, David was approached as an adult and enlisted to work *with* the teacher toward specific, respectable goals.

Eventually, David began to accept the reality of his position and a hopeful attitude toward bettering it. His need for achievement seemed to be taking precedence in his motivation, and his teacher abandoned the practice of trying to make all activities highly meaningful. Up to this point, David had worked only with shop-related words—their syllabication, spelling, and pronunciation—so that he would not be subject to "kindergarten stuff." His teacher was really working from the complex to the simple. David's specific weaknesses were not to be diagnosed and treated until he first became personally and meaningfully involved in the learning process.

It was two months before David really began the regular reading program—probably the most important two months of his life. David was better able to concentrate; his attention span had increased, and he was undergoing a basic personality change that was evident in all aspects of the program.

His instructor was hesitant about promoting David to the next level and allowing him to become involved in the vocational program. After six months, however, the change was made; and because of the extra effort of his teacher in personally contacting his new teachers, David did not regress. He continued to make good, steady progress. As an electronics assembler—a low-level entry course—David mastered the basic concepts required of him, passed on to radio, and eventually to TV repairman. The television course gave him plenty of anguish. Although he was familiar with the necessary vocabulary, he found the related math extremely difficult. Through persistence, 20 months after his entry into the Job Corps, he completed the course.

The half days spent in shop were not David's only area of success. He had applied himself diligently in the meantime to his general education course work and had attained a 6.5 reading level as measured by the Stanford Achievement Test, making him eligible for the G.E.D. high school equivalency program.

As two years is the maximum time a corpsman is allowed in the program, David became anxious over his uncertain future; several of his old objectionable characteristics began returning. He was counseled specifically to meet this crisis; and, with the aid of Atterbury's placement specialists, counseling guided him to enlist in the air force. His serenity restored, David again became very enthusiastic about the new life ahead.

He completed his G.E.D. one month before graduation, just meeting minimum ACE requirements. David, proudly wearing his "blues," made it a point to return to the center after basic training to look up his old friends and teachers. With the advantage of a little hindsight, he was more than appreciative for all that his Job Corps experience had done for him.

David's case is unusual; his success was almost fantastic. But the essence of his rewarding experience is not unusual. And it certainly need not be fantasy. For all the other Davids, branded failures in a school world bearing little resemblance to their perception of the real world, success is only as far away as the educational community's honest commitment to relevant service. There is no justification for tenth graders reading at a third grade level, nor for curricula that only frustrate students more each year. There is no justification for expecting students to handle advanced course work when we ourselves have failed to teach the 3 Rs.

It is already an old saw that personality problems and reading problems are interrelated, a downward spiral that, once begun, cuts a cycle of despair ever more deeply. Obviously, reading instruction alone could not be responsible for David's remarkable emotional improvement. Professional counseling certainly had to be involved and much attention given to the individual's specific difficulties in both reading and personality adjustment. But the point should not be missed that reading, our particular area of concern, is indeed of primary importance, not only in normal school progress and personality development but as a valuable, too often neglected tool for reversing the hard core pattern of failure. That it can be done has been illustrated by David. But it is not enough that we are able to help our Davids. Regardless of the immensity of our success, he must still carry the scars inflicted by his earlier experiences. How much better it would be to avoid producing case histories like David's and to provide, in the very earliest stages of the school career, instruction that is tailored to needs and recognizes uniqueness. This inflexibility *is* the crisis in education. Moreover, it is a challenge to the institution of reading instruction. All that remains is for us to meet it.

Imagine Tomorrow

Catherine E. White

FOR A MOMENT, I would like you to consider the words of John Lear, Science Editor of the *Saturday Review*:[1] "Among the animals of earth, only man can dream. Other species laugh and cry, love, rage, and kill. Man alone has the power to imagine tomorrow."

But, is it possible to imagine tomorrow when you are completely frustrated by a world whose doors are closed to you, apathetic because poverty and its attendant evils have robbed you of initiative and drive, psychically exhausted by the stresses of coping with a fruitless daily existence, and self-negating because repeated failures and rejections have conditioned you to more failure and rejection? I could not, I could only laugh and cry, love, rage, and kill.

Man must imagine tomorrow, and it must be made possible for every man to imagine tomorrow. We are concerned with tomorrow, and we are aware that tomorrow is here, now. We are also deeply concerned with the reading skills and their importance as a catalyst in releasing the vast human potential that is presently lying fallow or being wasted. We are all aware of the enormity of this problem and hope that as a result of our interchange of ideas and experiences, we will be able to return home with new knowledge, insights, and guidelines for positive action.

Today, reading skills are a critical element in every area of human endeavor and to every segment of society. Perhaps they may have the most relevance to those individuals who share two characteristics: being

[1] *Saturday Review*, 44 (September 2, 1961), 35.

out of school, whether as teenagers who have recently dropped out or as adults who never attended school, and being illiterate or functioning on such a low level as to be excluded from holding any but the most menial jobs. These are the individuals with whom the adult basic educators have been concerned for many years. Revolutionary changes have occurred in the field of adult basic education (ABE) over the past few years. A wealth of new approaches, methodologies, and materials has been developed and tried.

Exciting things are happening in ABE all over the country. ABE classes are attracting more and more students each year. Some communities now have set aside whole schools as adult education centers. One such institution is the Rochambeau School, the adult education center of White Plains.

White Plains, 25 miles north of New York City, has many of the same social, economic, and educational ills and ailments that are found in any urban setting.

White Plains has a long history of sound and consistent support of its schools and the residents of the community. It also has a long history of support of adult education. Its adult education program has operated continuously since 1922 and has had a full-time director since 1946. In the fall of 1964, the Rochambeau School, which had operated as an elementary school for many years, was closed as part of a widely applauded and successful plan for bringing about racial balance in the elementary schools. At this time federally sponsored manpower development training programs and basic education programs were just becoming available, and White Plains found itself in a unique position to initiate these programs. The board of education decided to reactivate the Rochambeau School as an adult education center. It was hoped that the establishment of an accessible, centralized facility would provide the means by which the unemployed and undereducated adult could upgrade his skills to job-entry level. Manpower development training and vocational programs were set up. ABE classes in schools scattered throughout the city were moved to Rochambeau. A day care center was set up so that ADC and welfare mothers could attend classes during the day.

At this time, the instructional pattern followed in ABE classes resembled in many ways that offered in the elementary schools. In most cases, child-oriented materials were used for the simple reason that nothing else was readily available. As might be expected, this parallel did not create an ideal learning situation. The publishing industry, however, had become aware of the need for action in this area. As a result of their widely attended New York symposium, several of the major publishing companies committed themselves to produce instructional materials specifically designed for the adult beginning reader.

Once such materials became available commercially, they were received

Imagine Tomorrow

by educators with interest. In 1965, under the leadership of A. T. Houghton and Joseph A. Mangano, plans were formulated for the establishment of a pilot project at Rochambeau. The Rochambeau Learning Laboratory evolved from these plans. The lab would utilize a variety of the new materials and techniques. It would also include facilities for providing instructional experiences tailored to the adult's intellectual and physical capacity, his attendance pattern, his goal expectations, and his psychological makeup.

The administrators at Rochambeau were farsighted and innovative men and women. They realized that there must be a total involvement of administrators, instructors, guidance counselors, neighborhood recruiters, and hopefully, students. The administrators had analyzed their target population and knew and understood its strengths and weaknesses. The planners knew the learning lab must provide a dramatically different approach because the majority of their students would have had wholly frustrating or defeating experiences with traditional methods of education. Also, the planners were innovative in that they chose to utilize a number of relatively untried instructional techniques and materials. A broad-based instructional approach would be needed because experience had indicated that most illiterate and functionally illiterate adults tended to progress at a relatively slow rate in the areas of reading and the other communication skills.

It was also realized that many of the students would be unable to utilize effectively any communication skills that might develop because of inadequate social living skills. Intensive attention, therefore, would have to be given to the practical areas such as consumer education, health and nutrition, occupational and social adjustments as well as to the more abstract areas of decision-making, self-realization, and self-actualization.

The creation and establishment of such an innovation immediately necessitated two moves. First, the neighborhood recruiters and guidance counselors would need orientation so that they could explain to prospective students that at Rochambeau there would be many ways to learn and that never again would a student be confronted with the futility of having only one book from which to learn—the more likely, with which to fail. The recruiters stressed that at Rochambeau, students would find a school in which they could succeed, a school whose staff was there solely to help them achieve their goals.

Second, a lab specialist would be needed. Inclusion of a wide variety of programed materials, overhead projectors, tape recorders, and other instructional devices required the services of a highly skilled individual to supervise and direct their use. The specialist's major responsibility would be to train, assist, and direct the classroom instructor to high levels of proficiency in using the instructional materials and devices in the most effective manner for the students.

During its first year of operation, prime consideration was placed on evaluating the degree to which the inclusion of these innovations accelerated the progress of students toward literacy. By the end of the year, certain trends had become apparent. ABE students did indeed react favorably to a lab environment, but not all of them reacted well toward some of the approaches. Many students enjoyed and showed good gains using self-directed and programed materials. Others balked at what they considered long hours of drudgery. It was observed that the students responded well to the teaching devices that had been used. The overhead projector and tape recorders were highly motivating and successfully utilized by many students. The innovations had definitely permitted more individualization, and selection of media based on student preference had contributed measurably to student involvement and interest. It was also evident that adults responded well to immediate feedback as it enabled them to identify their trouble spots and correct themselves. Elliott Lethbridge and John Kacandes, who were most closely involved with operation of the lab, felt that since general response had been positive, perhaps further expansion in these areas would be advisable. But, they felt, there must be sufficient allowance for interaction between teachers and students, between students and students, and between teachers and students and devices. Such interaction would be a critical factor in preventing dehumanization of the classroom.

In Fall 1967, there was further discussion with the Bureau of Continuing Education. Houghton, after consulting with instructional specialists on his staff who had surveyed the commercially available media and materials, recommended that the Rochambeau lab adopt and evaluate a recently developed total systems approach to the teaching of basic communication skills. This system provides sequential, integrated instruction in reading, listening, speaking, writing, and observing and in the thinking skills which underlie these acts. It was felt that this system would serve as the core instructional program but perhaps would be augmented if necessary by ancillary materials, instructional approaches, or media.

The focus of this system is on the development of the reading skills, since without the ability to read competently an individual is seriously disabled in any attempt to increase other skills. Careful analysis of the functional, perceptual, and interpretative aspects of the reading act had resulted in the inclusion in the system of techniques to provide direct and intensive instruction in the areas generally regarded as essential to reading competency.

The content in the system was developed to meet the needs of and to be relevant to the adult. In addition to the expected content-oriented materials, materials to develop social living skills are structured into the program. Enrichment materials are provided so that students will find learning entertaining and enjoyable, as well as informative.

Various media and modes are utilized to present concepts and ideas and to provide sufficient reinforcement so that even the very slow students are afforded ample opportunity to learn. Instruments, filmstrips, illustrations, and recordings, as well as a multitude of printed materials, are integrated into the components of the system.

The inherent interest and motivation provided by the variety of media insure a stimulating learning atmosphere. Heavy stress is placed on the use of audiovisual techniques because they offer the potential for maximum enrichment in a minimum amount of time. Instrument techniques are used to provide instruction in many skills because of the precision and control which they afford and because they provide the most effective and efficient medium for the presentation of a skill or concept. Its multimodal approach compensates for the relatively limited educational experience of the students and gives them the opportunity to utilize their preferred learning styles. Some learn more effectively through listening; some, through seeing; some, through writing; and some, through a combination of these modes. Inclusion of all modes of learning enables students to capitalize on their preferred style and to develop proficiency in modalities in which they are less proficient. The multilevel organization of the system allows a student to enter at his level of need and to progress at his own rate. The totally illiterate student is provided with readiness activities, and the partially literate student is provided with suitable activities and instruction at his particular level of need.

The many autoinstructional techniques increase involvement and learning time for each student by permitting him to respond to every question and exercise and by furnishing immediate correction and reinforcement. Personalized instruction is possible because the instructor is afforded time to work with individuals or small groups while the majority of students is involved in self-directing activities.

The system is organized in cycles of instruction which introduce and reinforce learning through a carefully planned sequence of activities. Each instructional cycle contains teacher-directed, self-instructional, and small- and large-group activities. Within each cycle, evaluation procedures are provided so that progress can be assessed both by student and instructor.

Once the decision to adopt the system had been made, the Rochambeau staff began the planning needed to make it operational. As the components of the system arrived and were set up in the lab, the atmosphere at Rochambeau began to crackle with excitement. What is that? Who will use this? How does that work? When everything was set up and in order, it was an impressive sight—but to some, perhaps a bit overwhelming.

The system had been adopted in the middle of the year, and superimposing any innovation on an existing structure generally results in a transition period during which there is some disturbance of routine, as there was at Rochambeau.

Immediate teacher orientation and training were needed. Since budget restrictions, among other things, limited after-hours activities, orientation was largely carried on during regular hours. All agreed this was not the most satisfactory arrangement. It would have been far better to conduct training at a time when all concerned could have devoted their complete attention to the task. Initially some of the teachers felt insecure at the thought of completely changing their methodology. The Rochambeau staff, however, working closely with the publisher's consultant, provided the instructors with an operational knowledge of the various instruments and instructional materials in a relatively short time. The staff and consultant also devoted much attention to providing guidance to the instructors in developing appropriate teaching styles for use with the system. The warm relationship that existed between the staff and the instructors was a prime factor in rapidly developing instructors who were at ease with the system.

The students were introduced to the system slowly. Each day a different technique would be introduced, explained, and demonstrated for them. Some, particularly the older students, initially seemed reluctant to change their habits and behavior patterns. Even such a small thing as changing seats upset several. However, the rapport and feelings of security which the staff had established served to allay any disquietude.

As Rochambeau settled into a new routine, certain things became evident. Students liked the change of pace; they liked using different instructional media, and they liked the increased opportunity for interaction with one another and with the staff. Instructors soon found that they were able to give more individual attention to those needing it because many students were operating independently much of the time. Instructors noticed that many students seemed to be developing more self-reliance and self-confidence. Some students indicated that their aspirational levels were rising. They talked about getting a job when they had finished the course or going on to prepare for high school equivalency.

Students generally were achieving and were showing more interest and involvement with learning. After several months it was evident that their motivation remained high. Anthony P. made a gain of nearly two years in five months and could not conceal his pride as he read aloud to the instructor or to his friends. Hosea D., who had gained slightly over three years in the same period, appointed himself as chief letter writer for one of the classes. He delighted in helping his classmates compose letters to friends, and the classmates welcomed assistance from a peer and took pride in his accomplishments.

Even with the assistance of the latest in educational technology, however, some students were not able to progress as fast as had been hoped. These students were typically at the readiness stage, were over forty, and generally had been receiving psychological or psychiatric therapy. Some were so emotionally insecure that they had trouble working independently and thus placed an extra burden on the instructor. Some, seeming to have a deep need for teacher-support, found it difficult to accept the auto-instructional techniques. Although those in this category progressed slowly according to standard measures, these students were showing progress in other ways. Even though progress was slow, their interest and enthusiasm were held, as evidenced by improved attendance. They began to interact more with other members of the class. They began to offer more comments and opinions during discussions. Some would even come to class when actually they should have been home in bed. One lady brought a vaporizer to use in class when she was suffering from a respiratory difficulty.

The Rochambeau Learning Laboratory has now been in operation for two and a half years and over 900 students have participated in its classes. It is difficult to assess what impact the lab has on the lives of its students and on the community. Based on an analysis of the past year, more students who temporarily had had to interrupt their learning because of crises returned to class on solution of their problems. The dropout ratio declined sharply. Students were starting school and staying to finish. The average daily attendance for each student markedly improved over that of the previous years. These are particularly significant trends when one considers that the typical ABE student's life consists of crisis after crisis: eviction, sickness, desertion, unemployment—all conspire to disrupt his life and prevent him from maintaining continuity with anything.

Two hundred and twenty-five students were followed closely over five months last year. Of these, 27 received sixth grade certificates which enabled them to register to vote; 13 received eighth grade certificates; 7 went on to high school equivalency classes; and 3 to vocational classes. Five welfare mothers sufficiently upgraded their skills so that they were able to accept jobs which enabled them to become partially or wholly self-sufficient. These figures are impressive in terms of human achievement.

Is it possible to assess the lab's impact on Julia B.? She began instruction six months ago. A month later she persuaded her employed husband to start night classes at the lab. He has been faithfully coming two nights a week ever since. And last month, Mr. B. brought another student to the lab—their teenage son who had dropped out of school. And what about Austin D.? He came to register at Rochambeau and wept in anguish as he explained that he could not hold a job because he had had only two years of schooling. He was ineligible for manpower training because of his low literacy level but was encouraged to begin basic education. Within six months, he had made such a spurt that he was transferred to manpower training during the day. He rearranged his life so that he could continue to come to the lab at night. He has since been graduated from manpower training and is employed as a machinist. But he is still attending night classes and now aspires to high school equivalency.

And is it possible to measure the effect of a grandmother whose success is transmitted to her grandchildren and inspires them to achieve in school? How do you measure the pride of families which come to graduation to see relatives receive their certificates? What does it mean to a child to have his parents now able to write a note to school explaining his absence? How does a man feel when he can read, understand, and fill out an application for a job? It cannot be measured.

Man alone has the power to imagine tomorrow, and Rochambeau is giving this ability to each student who passes through its doors.

Some Keys to Educational Parity

Omar K. Moore

Is IT SENSIBLE to hold the public schools responsible for the failures of inner-city children, or can school systems generally be held responsible for the success or failure of individual children of whatever class or economic level? The schools are being roundly attacked for the failure to teach basic reading skills to children of urban slums, but is this attack really completely valid?

I suggest that the schools alone are not responsible for the educational outcome—for the results achieved. Schools give assignments, but parents must help children carry the assignments out by providing appropriate home conditions and supports, including motivation especially. There must be a good deal of sharing, of collaboration, of interplay between the school and the home if the system is to work well. The educational process is a continuous one: it cannot be compartmentalized, and it cannot be scheduled so that learning goes on only during certain hours of the day and in certain settings. Both school and out-of-school experiences are natural and necessary complements. Perhaps two-thirds of the educational process takes place in the school and one-third, outside the school. The present school system will not be effective if that supportive one-third is not forthcoming.

Because of the economic and social problems confronting ghetto residents, ghetto parents usually do not have the time, the background, or the confidence to enable them to give their children assistance. Even though there is often a will, such parents are so severely limited by their living conditions and their own sense of inadequacy and despair, that they do

53

not even know how to begin. The sense of despair and inadequacy is cumulative—often over several generations; and apathy, born of desperation and hopelessness, sets in. Because of this absence of out-of-school contribution to the educational process, many children from ghetto families lose from three to four years between kindergarten and grade twelve. This is the penalty that ghetto children pay for not having the home assets which are expected to make our present educational system functional.

The three-to-four-year educational gap will not be caught up or closed within the present educational structure; for the cumulative effects of ghetto life, coupled with the growing need for greater skills to deal effectively with expanding knowledge and technology, only serve to widen the gap. The result is almost certain to become a losing fight which begins when basic skills are not mastered at an early age.

The problem thus becomes one not only of improving the formal in-school education but one of improving the out-of-school learning as well and of finding a feasible balance between the two—a mix designed especially for the ghetto child. This is no easy matter. We must be willing to try, singly and in combination, the widest possible range of programs that use all kinds of materials, people, and locations for education both inside and outside the school building. We must use tested methods in combination with experimental efforts. The problem is such that almost any innovation in the education of disadvantaged children makes some positive improvement if only by arousing parent interest and challenging teacher effort. The collective picture of all the things that have been tried so far is positive, but none of the innovations has been innovative enough. I use *innovative* to mean not only new teaching materials and methods but to include completely new departures in concept and program.

Before we can decide which types of innovation might help do a difficult job, we must look at what has been tried and see how well it worked. Are there programs that give promise, that have potential for real development? The first example, and perhaps one of the best, is Head Start. This is a positive program; it is good for children; it must be maintained and developed. Like other innovative programs it has accomplished some small good for the children it has reached, particularly as it has succeeded in arousing parent interest and hope. But it is not enough to overcome the setbacks the ghetto child will face as he progresses through the system. There have been some drawbacks: some ghetto mothers placed too great a burden on the Head Start program by expecting greater results than were actually forthcoming. Some mothers, believing that Head Start would do it better, even stopped the modest effort that they had been making to teach their children the alphabet or numbers.

What is probably needed is the development of sets of innovations, or programs, that provide sequences and progressions through which the home

Some Keys to Educational Parity

and the school together can provide the extra individual help now being provided the ghetto child—if at all—from some other tutorial source in the community. We need to parallel for the ghetto child the "fail-safe" aspects of the middle-class homes where the typical suburban parents become aware early that the child is having trouble in school and take steps to provide extra support and prevent failure. The fail-safe family is what makes the school system work well for so many middle-class children. Early awareness at home of appropriate achievement or signs of slippage is the first step.

Many people who set forth to try out innovations in the slums want the schools to do everything. Good intentions too often insulate the reformers from the perceptions that would prove most useful. Black parents in the inner city are now telling us that they want total control of the schools in which their children have not been learning. They are determined that they themselves will have a role from here on. They know that the schools cannot do the whole job within the school building and within the limitations of the school day. Even the exceptionally good teacher who tries to fill in, and be at once teacher and substitute for family involvement, is usually doomed to failure.

There are four kinds of educational models or systems:

- High risk, Low yield
- Low risk, Low yield
- Low risk, High yield
- High risk, High yield

We don't have any examples of the "Low risk, High yield" system; of the "High risk, High yield" variety there are very few indeed. High risk systems are characterized by the heavy use of technology. Parental involvement could raise considerably the yield in the low-risk systems. An early start in education—by four years old at the latest—could raise the yield in even the lowest risk systems. These are important keys to educational parity. Another is the increased use of paraprofessionals and others who can serve as surrogates for the ghetto family. Still another is the more extensive use of technology—such as television in the out-of-school and the preschool experience. We must start early to make the combined in-school and outside-of-school system more powerful. Above all, we must be ready to go the whole way with innovation if we really intend to have educational equality for the ghetto child. If we combine technology with people who care and if we find a way to reinforce the school and the home, I believe all children—in the ghetto and out—can successfully be taught to read.

Reading, Revolution, and Human Need

Philip H. Ennis

IT IS IMPORTANT to ruminate about the meanings of the words *revolution* and *reading* before we try to see how they go together. *Revolution* is a word almost emptied of meaning by its application to every conceivable change in the United States. I want to discuss briefly three situations which are more or less revolutionary and which are not only interrelated but also related to reading. The first is the position of the Negro in the United States. If there is any place in our society which has great revolutionary potential in the traditional sense, it is in the black community. But the story is not so simple as the updated Kerner Commission report would have us believe. It is too simple to say we are continuing to become two societies—one white and one black. The realities—both in political terms and in the facts of education, income, employment, migration, and housing—are more complex. A recent special census report (5) indicates that while the number of white families below the poverty line decreases significantly, the number of poor Negro families declines more slowly. And within New York, Chicago, and Los Angeles the number actually *increases* by over 20 percent. At the same time the proportion of Negro families making over $10,000 a year jumps dramatically from 7 percent in 1959 to 18 percent in 1967—a far greater percentage increase than among whites.

In education there is again the paradox of progress and retrogression. The median years of school completed among Negroes aged 25-29 increased from 11.4 in 1960 to 12.2 in 1968. White educational attainment remained unchanged. The proportion of Negroes who completed high school and are in college has risen impressively, but at this same time poor and Negro students *declined* in IQ scores and reading test scores as they progressed through school. I have a private theory about this drop: it is the familiar process wherein the compounded failure of reading skill and motivation over the school years is accompanied by an increasing reliance on reading—a surefire way to drive youngsters out of school.

The employment situation is the locus of even more complex and contradictory trends. While overall unemployment declined to new lows (4.3 percent for all central city residents), Negro teenager unemployment rose from 23 percent in 1960 to 30 percent in 1968. The theory that the best cure for Negro unemployment is an increasing growth rate for the whole society is seriously challenged by these figures. That there are persistent "structural barriers" to Negro employment now seems undeniable. Moreover, the fact that Negro-white pay differentials *increase* in jobs with higher educational requirements further undermines the commitment to education as the road to the mainstream. Ironically, this specific trend holds for Negro men *only*. Average salaries of Negro women are equal to, or sometimes higher than, those of white women—for both high and low occupational levels.

Finally, housing and migration patterns also show strange shifts. While more than half of the nation's 22 million Negroes now live in central metropolitan areas—about 12 million—the Negro influx into these areas has dropped dramatically. During 1960-1968 population in fringes around great metropolitan areas increased 28 percent, while population in central cities actually *declined* 1 percent.

Is the Negro community divided politically? Of course, but perhaps not in the obvious way one might think. A recent study (*4*) has shown that the more education a Negro has, the more likely he is to be tolerant and friendly toward whites. Yet at the same time, the more education he has, the more militant and active he is in the defense of Negro rights; and the more critical he is of the status quo. These facts, in conjunction with widespread housing segregation which holds higher-income and higher-educated Negroes in their middle class enclaves within or at the fringes of the ghettoes, could significantly reverse the historic fragmentation of the Negro community. The present disarray and polarization of black political movements may be only a pause before a political regrouping that reflects, in part, a genuine community of Negro interests and, in part, an ideological synthesis of implacable contradictions. Malcolm X is the prototype of the individual who can become the symbolic embodiment of such a regroupment. The impact of his life, transformations, his martyrdom, and his book merit serious thought.

Now for the second revolution, the one involving the constant subjection of almost every aspect of life, especially those aspects having to do with work and to the scrutiny aimed at increased rationalization and efficiency. This organized scrutiny is institutionalized in science and technology generally and their increasing utilization in the solution of older problems previously handled under the rubric of routine and tradition. The scope of this effort is impressive in dollar figures—Machlup (2) estimated a rate of about 11 billion a year in 1958 and a growth rate of 16 percent per year. Yet dollar amount is not the most important point.

The consequences of this enormous stream of new knowledge flowing into the economy are multifarious. I emphasize one point: the impact of new knowledge on the training and, specifically, the retraining of the work force. The changes in production and services rendered are under such continual modification that industry has had to develop an internal educational apparatus to keep its employees up-to-date. There are estimates that the average worker of today will have to be retrained three times during his career. And this retraining still appears to rely mainly on print, for scientific innovation has not spared reading itself from its purview. The result is a diverse and complicated set of teaching tools, ranging from the traditional journal, pamphlet, and book all the way to computerized programed instruction. The adult work force facing its continuing homework is to varying degrees illiterate.

The third revolution is more sociological. It is the changing social boundaries which define "we" versus "they"; the revolution is one which is changing the social roots of individual identity. At one time, if you knew a fellow's ethnic background, place of residence, and occupation, you could make a pretty good guess about his education, income, and religion. You could also guess fairly well about his style of life, political attitudes, and much of his social behavior. You could pretty well locate his overall social prestige and sense of identity. Today these close correlations among background characteristics have come unstuck. So has the relation between background and style of life. So, too, have the social bases of identity become less predictable. The so-called generation gap, the racial crises, the battle over education, suburb against city, the battles of one ethnic neighborhood against a rival ethnic neighborhood—all these indicate the social sloshing around that is caused by taking an old grid out of the ice cube tray when the ice is not quite ready.

Turning now to ruminating on the topic of reading, two cautionary notes are extended. The first is that one is likely to fall victim—because of his occupational commitments—to the fallacy of the "domination of the tool." Give a young child a hammer, and he thinks the world is for hammering; give him a saw, and he thinks the world is for sawing. Reading can do some things, but it will not set the world right. The ordinary good sense and modesty that exist most of the time with respect to the power of books and reading often give way to strident overstatement and overselling in a market where everybody else is similarly touting his wares.

But is the soft sell entirely useless? And is it possible that the accurately marketed product can survive?

Second, reading is such a protean activity and print is so diverse that it is quite important to acknowledge our ignorance of the basic social bookkeeping facts about who reads how much of what under what circumstances. We are even more ignorant about the basic processes of how readers are made, what sustains their reading in adult life, what gratifications and functions reading serves, and how it affects daily life on the job and at home.

More research is needed in adult reading—not in small, fragmentary, noncumulative, half propagandistic researches but in a carefully designed, large scale, conceptually informed study, or series of continuing studies.

It is clear that people read for a wide variety of reasons and for different reasons at different times. From a series of studies and surveys on reading patterns and reading in general, several main findings emerged.

First, the diversity of peoples' reading patterns described in 1942 by Ruth Strang still pertains today, but the extent to which reading spreads into the many facets of a person's life is far more complex than imagined. Readers tend to skip from one level to another—high to low—with regularity and ease. They read in many substantive areas—fiction and nonfiction, biography and social science, history and poetry. However, most readers stay away from some subjects. Second, people tend to read about what they know and believe in. Through a complex set of social and psychological processes, readers prescreen their books as they look for the familiar and avoid the unknown. The motivational basis for this conduct seems to lie in the fact that books are often used to sustain and support currently held views and feelings, and to explain and confirm deeply felt sentiments—both personal and social. Another major motivational reason for this selectivity is the use of reading for practical, pragmatic, and instrumental ways. This is perhaps one of the most thoroughly institutionalized uses of print in our society dating back at least to the 1830's when how-to-do-it books were as basic a part of the publishing scene as they are now.

Another reason to read stems from interest in one's job or community activities. A ubiquitous and powerful motive for reading is to escape, if only for a moment, from oneself, from one's responsibilities, and from those holes in the daily fabric that might let in the sounds of emptiness or disorder.

Let us turn now to the implications for reading stemming from the continual growth and spread of science and technology. Even if the information explosion is only a paper explosion, its effects ramify individual lives and threaten to overload the present institutional arrangements in industry, in government, and in our educational system. An inadvertent consequence is that science and technology are producing illiterates in a wide band of occupations: consider the insurance salesman who has to unlearn the techniques used in years of hard selling a limited set of policies in order to learn—often with help of programed manuals—how to service his clients' many financial and investment problems; or the weary city planner who has to read the journals and the books in five or six social sciences as well as the mountain of technical data coming from local and federal reports; or those of nonscientific occupations who are having to learn new languages and new ideas. And if it is hard on those adults, it is even harder on those parts of the social structure that have been traditionally in charge of either the dissemination of print or its compression and translation. Part of the response of these institutions, as well as of industry, has been to build a wall of credentials around jobs. "You can't possibly do this job without a high school diploma or college degree," say personnel managers about jobs that might well be handled with less education. After all, doesn't experience from World War II, when almost every warm body was put in a war plant (called defense plant), suggest that one can dispense with credentialism when pressed? In part, credentials serve as an indicator that an applicant probably has the stick-to-it skills and docility required of the work force—but only to an unknown degree and, to my guess, a relatively small degree. Do such credentials guarantee that the applicant will be able to meet the employer's needs for continuing relearning? Currently industry is putting vast and increasing expenditures into the reeducation of its employees. Thus, reeducation is necessary to handle the successive waves of illiteracy following each scientific and technological advance.

There are other areas in which there are either no institutions of relearning or very weak ones at best, such as the public library and the newspaper. While some newspapers, some journalism schools, and some libraries are attentive to the necessity of becoming "institutions of translation" to bridge the literacy gap between public and scientific advances that bear on everyday life, most are not.

The pressure to read for practical purposes can be so heavy and can become so onerous due to the training of "how to read a page" in school that the use of print for other motives can be endangered.

As for the black revolution and how it is affecting reading, let me begin with the simplification—but empirically grounded simplification—that everyone identifies himself as a reader or a nonreader simply as an aspect of personality that is independent of identification as a man or woman, employed or unemployed, high school graduate or dropout. Readers see themselves as different from nonreaders, as illustrated by the woman who said, "You see, I have a mixed marriage. I am a reader and my husband is not."

Reading, Revolution, and Human Need

From surveys we found that among people who graduated from high school there are twice as many readers as among those who didn't finish. While this fact is no surprise in a general way, it is devastating when looked at more closely. The following data compare graduates and non-graduates and the proportions who read early in their lives (before the end of formal education) and those who read now as adults. Those who read at both times, early and at present, can be called "regular" readers. Those who read early in their lives but have given up reading as adults can be called "deserters." Those who read now but did not when young are "late starters." Those who read or have read at neither time are "non-readers."

EDUCATIONAL DIFFERENCES IN READING

		High School or More						Less than High School		
		Early Reading						Early Reading		
		Yes	No					Yes	No	
Current Reading	Yes	47%	18%	65%		Current Reading	Yes	19%	11%	30%
	No	20%	15%	35%			No	28%	42%	70%
		67%	33%	100% = (779)				47%	53%	100% = (686)

The data show that among those who finished high school, the number of people who were readers early in life but do not read as adults was replaced with approximately the same number of people who didn't read when young but who became readers as adults. In other words, there are as many deserters to reading as there are late starters. Among those with less education than high school, not only is the core of regular readers smaller but there are about three times as many deserters as there are late starters. The significance of this matter is that among the less educated, and more certainly among the poor black and white in the urban slums, if a youngster doesn't start as a reader, it is unlikely that he is going to pick it up later. And the tragedy is that the urban schools for black children are failing to produce readers. There is some evidence that among the most depressed Negroes a large proportion of those who finished eight grades cannot pass reading tests at the fifth grade level—the boundary of functional literacy. A dramatic case in point is the story that Malcolm X tells in his autobiography. He was so frustrated in his attempt to write a letter to Elijah Muhammad that he got a dictionary and painfully taught himself to read by first copying the words, page after page and then reading everything he could get his hands on. He makes a significant statement about his difficulties (3).

In the street I had been the most articulate hustler out there—I had commanded attention when I said something. But now trying to write simple English I not only wasn't articulate, I wasn't even functional. How would I sound writing in slang the way I would say it, "Look, daddy, let me pull your coat about a cat, Elijah Muhammad.

And Malcolm finished the eighth grade. What is the extent of this failure among black youngsters, and why does it occur? I don't think conventional wisdom has the answers, but I am sure that the American educational plant is a successful producer of illiterates. The costs involved are great in terms of direct loss of productive manpower and even greater in the indirect costs of remedial action—including costs from the welfare and prison systems, the two great nonremediers. But in human terms the loss is incalculable. Reading may not be the only way for people to use their history and literature to forge a strong social and personal identity, but it is one way and a way denied millions of people. The remedies are difficult to implement, if indeed they are known, mainly because the acts are committed by well intentioned people. It is those very good intentions that insulate the perception of what it is all about.

The significance of reading for identity might be made more vivid and personal if I quote from one of our interviews with a Negro lady, college educated, mother of five sons, married to a chemist, and herself a medical research assistant.

I think books concerning Negroes that I started to read in the last few years of high school and early college years (were most important to me) because those books, you just don't have around the house, and there was nobody talking about them being in the library . . . they didn't teach them to you in school . . . it was a source of amazement to me to find out all these things. I think that these books have played a great part in helping my thinking. . . . The title of one was *Amos Fortune*. He was a Negro . . . it was about somebody who really lived and attained his freedom. Of course, you know, we were taught about Booker T. Washington and Frederick Douglass; but, I mean, they just didn't seem so real, you know, as some of the people I found out about later . . . who really did the things that anybody else would do under the same circumstances. It's sort of seeing different. Before that you didn't think in terms of yourself as being a Negro, you know, really Negro. You were just somebody else. *Amos Fortune* told of how he came here . . . the things he went through . . . how he felt and how he thought. He worked . . . and he knew that after he'd worked a certain length of time and made a certain amount of money and learned a trade, that he would be free. And so he was, and then he married; but then he had community problems. He wasn't accepted. But he still worked, and he made a living for his wife. It was just an ordinary life, and how he lived and managed and all. And he was a real person. I knew there was supposed to be people like that at that time, but it was very difficult for me to think in terms of Negroes being anything except slaves. I knew it was factual that there were supposed to have been landowners, Negroes who owned slaves, and all that kind of business, but (pause) I don't know. It just did something for me. It started me to thinking, helping me to think in certain areas. It even helped to bring about some real understanding. Now we used to live in Kentucky, in school we used to have Negro history week like they have here, but after the Negro history week was over, you know, there just wasn't any more, you know. It was almost like studying about somebody else and not about my own people. It could very well have been because there weren't books available to give you more understanding, and I didn't even know that books were available until I went to college, and I started to find out about some of these books. About people outside of some of these standard ones they tell you about—like Frederick Douglass, Booker T. Washington, and Marion Anderson. It helps to find out that you really have some people, and they lived someplace, and they came from someplace, and they did things like other people, and you just didn't start from right here.

The point here is that black identity is a step toward human identity. Unfortunately, some people see the formation of black identity as the destination; too few see it as a *necessary* step on the journey toward the attainment of human identity.

Notes and References

1. Ennis, Philip H. *Adult Reading in the United States,* National Opinion Research Center, University of Chicago, Report 106, 1965, 35.
2. Machlup, Fritz. *The Production and Distribution of Knowledge in the United States.* Princeton, New Jersey: Princeton Press, 1962, 370.
3. Malcolm X. *The Autobiography of Malcolm X.* New York: Grove Press, 1966, 171.
4. Marx, Gary. *Protest and Prejudice.* New York: Harper and Row, 1967.
5. "Trends in Social and Economic Conditions in Metropolitan Areas," Series P-23, No. 27. Washington, D.C.: United States Government Printing Office.

Reactions to Reading, Revolution, and Human Need

HENRY SPRINGS: I found Ennis' paper both provocative and relatively complete. But no one in education or the social sciences expects pat answers to the complex problems we face. When problems are posed, alternatives should be offered. It seems to me that a scholar's primary service to the practitioner is to delineate carefully the problem and offer a wide range of alternative courses which the practitioner may realistically discuss and consider.

Ennis has admirably described our threefold revolution and the paradoxical movement of white and black in education, in employment, and in political posture. Certainly, the scientific and technical revolution described demands that the schools attend to educating young people for lifelong learning or retraining. However, I am not completely certain that I understand the social revolution described as the one which is changing the social roots of individual identity. If anything, ethnic background, address, and job are more powerful tools to stereotype than before. The black man living on Lake Shore Drive in Chicago and working in an office in the Prudential Building is an Uncle Tom to the black man living in the blight of Lawndale or Grand Boulevard. To the Appalachian white living up-town and working for Work-A-Day, the Jewish storekeeper who lives on the North Shore is Shylock. And so it goes.

If by social sloshing around Ennis refers to the dilemma of the white liberal or the black who still favors integration, then I do see a loss of social identity. These people find it difficult to accept or react to attacks from the left. Yet in good conscience they cannot identify with the right and middle of the road. And the middle of the road is to them a cop out. However, with respect to the other kinds of social identity, it seems to me that we are still a nation of ethnic groups, that the melting pot never really did melt. The strength of our political system has been its respect of and attention to the pluralism in our population.

Ennis accuses our nation's schools of being successful producers of illiterates. Others have accused us of producing technically competent barbarians, of not placing enough emphasis on academics, or of placing too much emphasis on preparation for going to college. We are accused, in the area of reading, of not doing enough and of a lack of emphasis on literacy. Now Ennis accuses us of too much emphasis—the hard sell of reading. He recommends that we use a soft sell approach: that reading as an accurately marketed product can survive.

It seems to me, to use Ennis' language, that in order to market a product accurately one needs an early and complete knowledge of the consumer's needs and demands; a trained sales force sensitive to these needs; and familiarity with the product, the territory, and the processes of production. We can manufacture a wide variety of shoes to fit every foot because we know how to make the shoes and we know how to train the salesmen to sell them. But do we really educate our customer contact people, our teachers, to be sensitive to the needs of the learner? And even if we do, do we give that teacher the opportunity to establish the same one-to-one relationship the salesman forms with the customer? And realistically, can one institution sell shoes and provide psychological counseling, custodial services, social functions, community participation, and aesthetic appreciation?

Perhaps it can but not without some drastic restructuring and retraining. What assistance can the schools expect from the colleges and universities who train the salesmen? Academics may know the product. They may know what the general trends of demands are. But do they really know the territory, the social dynamics of a school in its community? It is not enough to say that the schools must do a better job, for, as Ennis so aptly says ". . . good intentions can insulate perceptions of what it is all about."

We need help from our scholars, from our citizens, from our government. We need to know in order of priority what we want our schools to do. We need autonomy at the local level to accomplish these things. We need research to tell us which approaches best sell the product. What we need least is criticism without involvement or suggestions for possible courses of action.

Now, how do we assist our children to discover the satisfaction reading can bring? How do we get them to expend the effort it takes to learn to read well before they fully understand the rewards this expenditure will have?

NANCY PONSONBY: Reacting from the elementary school level, I find that I tend to agree with Ennis' idea of overselling the product. We are batting from right and left, "Read, read, read; you will never get anywhere if you don't read." I think this approach forms frustration in the child. You know when you have to do something and you don't seem to have the proper tools to do it, the task is far more difficult.

Sometimes reading can be a natural act for the child. When he comes into school, a child can learn to read from his own words. I don't think we have to worry about nonstandard, substandard English, or dialects. If we use them in teaching the child how to read, it becomes more of a natural act than batting at him constantly, "You must learn to read." Instead of building an environment to make materials adequate for the ghetto child or disadvantaged child, let's use his environment; let's use his language and teach him from that end.

I also react positively to Ennis' remark that people tend to read what they know about and what they believe in. This opinion fits into the same theory with these children.

I believe that the language the child brings to school with him *is* the child. If we reject that language to build experiences for a new language, then we are rejecting that child. I don't see how we can get anywhere that way. As the child grows, we must not just say he has learned to read and let it go at that. I think we have to sustain this interest in reading. We must have far more materials with which these children can identify.

When we reject the language, we are rejecting that child's self-identity. When we feed him books that do nothing for his identity, then we again are rejecting that identity; and we are fighting our own cause.

Children should be involved in book selection. Through paperback programs and through magazines, we can get children to choose what they want to read. Sometimes book selection in the library becomes book censorship in the library; that is, to a child, you are censoring his reading material when you put books on a shelf and say, "This is what you have to choose from." This isn't the way to develop a lifelong interest in reading, and reading is very important.

SAMUEL STRATTON: I represent that World War I lost generation. I am a reactor; but I guess, more importantly, I am also a subject of the things you have been talking about and thinking about.

We are in a crisis, as our scholars have indicated; and if we aren't careful, we shall be frustrated by that crisis. We are desperately looking for answers: not just looking for answers, but desperately, almost frantically, looking for answers. If we ask the right questions, perhaps we can find the right answers. I am not certain that we are asking the question that seems to me most pertinent. That question is "What is the end of education?" Is there a guiding philosophy of education any more?

I was pursuing and still am pursuing not social identity but self-identity. And the social scientists are not asking the right question because they are overemphasizing social identity. It may be that I am just confused with these terms; but as I hear them developed, I am not impressed that their inquiry is addressed to self-identity. Sociologists seem to stress the *we* and *they* more than the *I*. We must have *I*'s, literally and figuratively. Reading tools, subject matter, and curriculum are not really basically essential. People are.

One thing I loved about Booker T. Washington was his saying, "Early in my life I decided I could not know books, so I decided to know men. I made men my books."

Study people, people, people.

MARGARET BURROUGHS: The attitudes of many people bother me: people who write books and who have been writing books; publishers who have been publishing books and who until the past four or five years did not consider the material concerning black people or other minority people in this country as a thing that would make money. Then all of a sudden there is great interest because people have discovered gold in "them thar hills." I wonder how much of this change is really a sincere desire to do something to inspire children to read meaningful material—the wonderful

Reading, Revolution, and Human Need

stories not only of black people in this country but of white people also—
or whether it is purely having an eye for profits.

The other thing I would like to comment on is this matter of identity, and
I would relate identity to self-identity in the same way Stratton relates it.
I remember in school—elementary, high school, college—I was a fairly
bright kid, I guess. I liked to read. But so much of what I was reading—
Dick and Jane and all those things about father going off to the office and
mother staying home and keeping the house—had no meaning for me. My
father didn't have any office; my mother couldn't stay home; she had to
go out and work. She did domestic work in Hyde Park. I was able to read
those stories. You put up with them. But it was only when somewhere along
the line the teacher or the book would mention something about black
people, that all of a sudden there was an electric light bulb that just stuck
in my mind and I was alert. This pattern went on all through high school
and even through college. I could put up with all the rest because I had
to get an education. But it didn't really spark any fires in me.

Suppose there had been much more of this material, not only for me
but for other young people—black or white, Puerto Rican, or Mexican.
Suppose this same thing had been done for the Mexican child to enable
him to find out something about himself.

ROMAN PUCINSKI: One of the luxuries that I believe you social scientists
enjoy, which we politicians cannot enjoy, is that you are able to deal in
the abstract. We have to try to zero in on the immediate problem and then
try to translate it into meaningful legislation and popular support by those
who elect us.

I read the paper presented by Ennis, and I listened with great interest
to the discussion. As chairman of the subcommittee on general education,
I work with this problem almost constantly. Today's subject could be
divided into two parts. The first part, and one that very much concerns us
in Washington, is the ability of people to read. You really can't address
yourself to the question of reading and human needs if people can't read.

One of the things that concerns me deeply is the tendency, even at this
late date, to really not address yourself to the fundamental basic problem
of lack of reading ability. While we hear a great deal about it, have
conferences, and spend a great deal of time lamenting it, we have seen
technology move forward with all sorts of new techniques and devices in
machinery (the reading typewriter and various other things); yet we still
find in survey after survey that youngsters are reading substantially below
reading grade level, and without the comprehension they must have if they
are to learn.

This result indicates to me that we are not giving children the right
combination of tools to provide inspiration in the classroom and above all,
the right kind of teacher who can motivate.

Three years ago we held hearings in Washington on the nature of the reading material that young people get in school. We had to make very clear that we were not in any way injecting ourselves in the role of censors, but we did feel that our committee could become a forum, a vehicle for an exchange of ideas where we could spotlight the tensions on this whole subject. So far as we could ascertain, it had not been done before. When we talked about reading and human needs, reading and better understanding, and reading as the vehicle for people to understand one another, we were rudely awakened to find that our books completely lacked any material on the minority groups in this country. It was apparent to us that, at that time, the textbooks of this country were dominated for the most part by the white, Anglo-Saxon, Protestant element. There was little mention of the huge contributions made by the various minority groups in this country.

One of the great dilemmas that confronted our committee was that we are a polyglot nation. No other nation in the world is as heterogeneous as we: a nation composed of a tremendous number of ethnic groups, nationality groups, religious groups, and racial groups all working together, living together, and moving forward together. And yet as one looked into the textbooks of this country, he could find only scant reference to this particular phenomenon. This situation has been improved now.

I have always felt that this composition was one of the great strengths of our republic. We have demonstrated here that people can to a lesser or greater degree get along, even though they are of different religious and ethnic backgrounds and heirs to different social values. And yet, nowhere do the books that our children read in class allude to these points. The impression of the American Negro, for a couple of generations, was symbolized by "Little Black Sambo." Somewhere along the line you would read that there was a fellow named Pulaski who participated in the American Revolution; maybe you might even throw a von Steuben or Kosciuzko in somewhere; and of course, there is a large Italian community in this country, so maybe you heard a little bit about Galileo.

What I am trying to point out is that if we are going to meet the human needs of this country through reading, the publishers and all those who control education locally ought to recognize that this is a polyglot nation and that it has become as big as it is simply because we found an ability to work with one another. This is a never ending revolution, and one that is finding new meaning and new expression every day.

VIRGINIA H. MATHEWS: It seems to me that we have been talking about the importance of reading for the sheer joy of it.

Several people have said compulsion breeds frustration. I know that Pucinski is the first one to know that along with the ability to read—

that is, the skill building—there needs to be the motivation and the access to a rich variety of things to read.

As Stratton pointed out, people need to go along to introduce the books.

SAMUEL STRATTON: Reading is important. Who would deny that? And reading skill is important. But what you are reading is so much more important. I am seriously disturbed about what we are reading. The ability to read, the ability to manipulate life and society, is certainly not evidence of greatness nor goodness. Are we concerned only with the intellectual charlatanism of manipulation?

Again, let me emphasize ends. I am only a very faint echo of John Dewey. Please let me emphasize that we must socialize the child. But, it is such an intricate process.

Kenneth Kluck in "Prejudice and Your Child" reports the following incident which took place in a New England school that had a reputation for good race relations. When a teacher was assembling her third grade class after play period in the school yard, the children did not want to stop playing and return to their classroom. The teacher was somewhat impatient in gathering the stragglers. One little boy returned breathlessly to the line just as it started to move away. It was clear that he had been playing rather hard, and his face was covered with dirt from the playground. The teacher looked at him and shouted, "Jimmy, look at you. You are all dirty. You look just like a little colored boy." There were two Negro children in that class, and the other children laughed at Jimmy. These two children hung their heads in embarrassment and shame.

Unfortunately, such incidents are not rare. A teacher in a New York City public school considered it desirable to separate the children in her class according to an estimate of their academic standing. Because this school is in a mixed neighborhood, she had white, colored, and Puerto Rican children in the class. Almost invariably the white children were placed in the first rows; the Negroes, in the middle rows; and the Puerto Rican children, in the back rows. The teacher insisted this procedure was in no way a reflection of racial attitude, and she did not believe that the children in her class could be influenced by this pattern.

For the record, I believe that all children can be taught to read. I have seen no child that I did not believe could be taught. But we must have the right attitude toward the child; we must have faith in the child and faith in ourselves. Unless we can take the democratic leap of faith, we cannot find meaning and direction for ourselves.

HENRY SPRINGS: Moore, in his keynote speech, stated that the ability to read rests with those primary teachers of the three- and four-year-olds.

I think this fact is highly evident under a Title I project we have on the west side of Chicago. We call it the Child-Parent Clusters. These are small schools; there are six or seven on the west side. They are portable type schools, air conditioned classrooms on wheels, clustered together.

There are a principal, five or six teachers, several teacher aides, and student helpers. There are 75 to 80 three- and four-year-old children. The thing that makes it successful is that if the child enrolls, the parent must enroll. The mother must come in every day. The father may come two or three times a week for instructional sessions.

These schools have been in existence for the past two years, and their success is unbelievable. Children finish that one year and are ready for kindergarten. The reading readiness scores are where they should be. We have very few failures. Usually, the failures are because of emotional problems or other problems that can eventually be worked out.

I think that one of the answers to the problem of reading is that we must involve parents.

On the west side of Chicago is a large and most difficult high school with 5,200 students and 232 teachers. It is in a teeming area that went up in smoke last spring. We have some factions over there fighting and carrying on and making it most difficult to run a high school. We have the problem of 1,700 or 1,800 1-B's, freshmen, coming into the high school every September. Their average reading score is perhaps fourth to fifth grade ability. They are thrown into classes. They are given textbooks which they can't read.

We are trying many things. We have the educational equipment and laboratories; we have special reading teachers and consultants coming in to try to help; and we have what is known as a continuous book fair. Paperbacks, magazines, and books are in every classroom and in the library.

The students run the book shop, and they sell the books as fast as we can purchase them. They will go into the library and purchase *Black Rage, Black Power, Malcolm X,* and everything else that is published on the black man. Some of the youngsters can't read these books, but they carry them around with them all the time. Maybe they are assimilating some of the information through osmosis. But if you ask them about these books, they will be able to tell you something about them.

I often make a point of approaching them to ask, "What did you learn about this book? What are you learning here?" As somebody is telling about the books, others are listening. And the interest is there.

Many of the students have enrolled in the educational reading classes. We keep those reading labs open from eight o'clock in the morning until ten at night, and the students come in. They ask for help. This activity may be an inroad into this problem of the inability to read; but if we could get the parents involved in this type of thing, we would have greater success. My district superintendent is trying. We have district parent meetings. There are eighteen elementary schools and one high school in this district, and parents come out. Usually three to four hundred parents attend these meetings, and we discuss problems that are pertinent to the area.

But I think that the key lies with the three- and four-year-old child. After a boy or girl reaches the third grade, after he finishes those primary years, if he hasn't acquired reading skills, he is going to have a difficult time from then on.

NANCY PONSONBY: Then you are saying that instead of making up for the involvement of parents with a program such as Moore spoke of, you bring the parents in and involve them instead. You instruct them and teach them to help the child at home.

HENRY SPRINGS: I think this approach is the only answer.

ROMAN PUCINSKI: We have had some excellent results in this direction in the Adult Education Program. In Kentucky recently at some hearings, we were absolutely amazed at the results being obtained with adult education programs that involve the school, parents, and the children. We found people driving decrepit old cars—fifteen, twenty miles twice a week—just to participate in these programs.

I might add one little footnote to what Springs has said. He didn't say it because he is modest; but the programs that he has at Marshall High School obviously are producing some phenomenal results because, despite all the problems he mentioned, the fact remains that better than 50 percent of the youngsters in his school graduate and go on to college. Now that is a high percentage when you consider the problems and the various other factors involved.

This fact indicates to me that we have been operating under a lot of myths. I think that, given the tools, the inspiration, and the leadership in school, the disadvantaged child will make progress and will go on to higher education. For decades we wrote that child off and said, "Let's just do the best we can with him until he is sixteen, and then push him out."

Here is a man who did not accept that doctrine, and the results are apparent when he has better than 50 percent of his graduates going on to college.

MARGARET BURROUGHS: I find myself concerned about the attitude of some new, young teachers coming into schools in the black communities. I don't know where they are getting these attitudes—I suppose out of teachers' colleges and universities but these newcomers have the attitude that the child in the black community or the ghetto child (meaning black) is somehow inherently different. They seem to feel he is a different species of human being and is limited in his ability to learn certain things.

I think it is the responsibility of teachers to teach. And if English is our language, all children—black children, Italian children, and everybody else—should be taught English, not the language they come to school with. Now certainly we know that in the homes of the various nationality groups a sort of relaxed language is spoken, using some words of our folk language that are acceptable. But I feel that all children should be taught *our* language. And I feel that all of our children, unless incapacitated physically or mentally, can learn to read and can learn to love reading. I really resent these people who water down the curriculum for the black community and who do not set their sights as high as they should. I think the sights should be as high as the sky. A teacher must really try, and if something doesn't work the first time, try, try, try again. That is the meaning of the word motivation.

ROMAN PUCINSKI: I believe there is ample evidence to indicate that a black child is just as capable of absorbing the learning process as the white child, given all other factors of an equal nature. We have conducted studies in schools where black youngsters have progressed just as well as white children. So the lady is absolutely correct; there has been a tendency by educators to try to water down the curriculum into an inferior curriculum in the black community which has a psychological impact on the young people and has a tendency to continue and perpetuate the myth of inferiority.

NANCY PONSONBY: I also agree wholeheartedly with Burroughs. I did not say that the curriculum should be watered down. I think that any child, regardless of color, should be taught from his own language.

I am a believer in the language experience approach to reading. I think that children should speak their own language and see it written down. The folk language of the child should be written down, and the child should learn to read that language first.

I also think that all children should be able to speak English as *English*. And I know that there is a range in a classroom of black children just as there is in a classroom of white or integrated children. I just think that all children should be taught from their own language.

MARGARET BURROUGHS: I still don't know what you mean by "their own language." The folk language that is used at home they know already, so that doesn't have to be taught.

NANCY PONSONBY: They don't need to be taught their language but they should be taught to read through that language.

In the language approach to reading, when a child comes to school he dictates stories to the teacher. The teacher then teaches him to read through the stories he dictates. I have used this approach in classrooms where I have taught, and it works beautifully. The language, grammar, or English may not be perfect, but the use of his language makes it easier for the child to learn to read.

OMAR K. MOORE: There seems to be general agreement on the part of the various panel members that regardless of where we apportion blame or praise, we cannot expect major improvement in the educational process unless something is done to involve parents in relevant ways.

Especially in the ghetto areas or where you have three or four years to make up in terms of overall outcome in the school system, I think that in order to achieve anything like parity it is going to be necessary to train a good many paraprofessionals from the local community.

In other words, I do not think, and I want to be clear about this, that the involvement of the parents alone will do. These black paraprofessionals, who themselves need not have completed high school and whose own reading may be very weak, must be part of this process of self-identity on the part of the children. I think it is important for children in the black ghetto to understand that, in addition to their parents, there are other black people who care.

I would say that Cohen's program in Talent Corps is pertinent here. Her program offers a way both to get the advantage of utilizing paraprofessionals and to draw them into the school system. The school system is going to have to be modified in various ways, not only by the greater involvement with parents, but with local paraprofessionals also.

The teacher is going to find herself—whether she be black or white—acting more like a professional, helping out, and being a supervisor with respect to directing a much more complex operation than has traditionally been the case. We do need some structural changes in the school.

One more thing about parent identification. If any of you do take the trouble to read some of the things our group has published, you will find that we try to keep the parents out of our laboratory while their own child is in the program. We have black parents come to our laboratory all through the year. They can come in. We want them in. We want them to know the processes. We want them to become involved. But to say that they are involved is not the same thing as to say they are put in the position to directly superintend the actual learning of their own particular child.

When by accident this situation occurs, you see a disappointed mother or a too proud mother. There is a point about giving the child some protection to learn to make mistakes. For instance, we make specific provisions to protect the child from the overeager or the angry parent who keeps the child from exploring freely or trying things out. In other words, it is possible to involve the parents and local paraprofessionals, and still provide an area within the laboratory and/or laboratory school where the child has a few minutes a day to himself without severe censorship and without feeling that everything he is doing is being monitored by someone who can distort what he has done. Sometimes advice to keep parents out really doesn't mean that the professionals don't want parents to be involved; it means, rather, parents aren't wanted in the detailed machinery on a day-to-day basis in such a way as to take freedom away from the child. We are going to need a massive infusion of paraprofessionals from the local communities. Cohen's program describes excellent use of both paraprofessionals and parents.

My last point is directed to the congressman because we don't always have a congressman close at hand. Since I have been a persistent critic of so many things that were well intentioned but didn't work out, I think it is really time for the congressmen to go beyond their own maze of experts and look directly at ongoing programs. Many of us warned our congressmen about Head Start's not really giving an academic head start, but I don't know whatever happens to these criticisms. They never seem to reach the right targets.

I noticed that Pucinski mentioned my own program, the Talking Typewriter. Here is one little, miserable device representing our program which somehow came to the attention of his committee, and yet the people who used the device knew that it was a research instrument and was not meant to be a general solution. We are not represented with the instrument. In other words, that particular piece of mechanical device got separated from the program, separated from the people who are really using it, and reappeared in a congressional hearing or in their investigatory processes out of context. And this type of thing happens over and over again.

Concluding Observations

LEO FAY: From the preceding papers and discussions, I would like to consider three or four significant points.

Two or three times we heard that we are in danger of overselling reading. For example, Ennis made this statement. Mann pointed out that we should be aware of the fact that reading is not always a prime prerequisite for learning. And he went on to make the point that youngsters do, in fact, learn in many ways and that we might be guilty of overemphasizing learning to read, particularly with young children.

I would like to balance these particular ideas against what I thought was the main thrust of Rutledge's presentation: that while reading may not necessarily be a prerequisite for learning, it certainly is a prerequisite for successful living in our society. He pointed out what the manpower needs of this nation are at the present time and what they will be within the foreseeable future. As school people, we ought to take pride that today's accomplishments are built upon the past successes of the schools. And it is our success today and tomorrow that will build the future of this country.

Literacy is basic to all of this matter. Rutledge indicated that we are moving into an era of human resources used to manipulate the computer and the machines. The electronic miracle that is taking place at the present time is really only an extension of the human brain, and the human component and the human resource that we have to develop relate to higher levels of literacy. Thus, we might be in a position to issue a statement to Congressman Pucinski and the Perkins Committee on Education and Labor in the House, and the Yarborough Committee in the Senate suggesting that reading be given a high priority for all of the youngsters in this country, a statement emphasizing that we can no longer tolerate a sizable proportion of functionally illiterate people in our society.

Moore suggested that all youngsters probably could be taught to read successfully. We have other evidence to substantiate this point of view; we can suggest in terms of points and papers that this is a high priority area for the educational system of our country.

The second point is that we ought to be more concerned with the content of what youngsters read. In the long run, when we are concerned with the development of higher levels of literacy for children, whether in first grade or in graduate school, content is of greater significance than a particular method or a particular set of materials. This point might be expanded in one of the IRA journals. It is a point which ought to be of concern to curriculum and supervision people. It is also a point of significance to librarians. It certainly is a point of significance to publishers: that when we put together materials which have as their prime purpose the teaching of the basic skills of reading, we must be concerned with the content as well as the skills that are to be developed.

The third point, which I consider quite significant, is the idea that the educational process and the educational outcome, the products of our schools, are both affected by more than the school alone. Moore addressed himself very directly to this point, and Henley also stressed it.

Several times we have heard of the significance of paraprofessionals, and we have had a heavy emphasis here upon the human component in successful teaching and learning. Interestingly enough, there are still states that have laws against the use of paraprofessionals. We have school people—administrators and teachers, too—who are concerned lest this be a way of downgrading the teaching function in the classroom. I think that we ought to take a good hard look at this area as mentioned by Stratton, a man who obviously has a deep sense of what education is, and a deep feeling for what teachers are really all about. He finished one of his remarks with "People, people, people."

We saw the work that is being done in New York City, bringing women from ghetto areas into a college program which prepares them to serve in a variety of educational, health sciences, and social welfare agencies.

In Indianapolis we have a program in 23 inner-city schools involving almost 200 paraprofessionals. It is a fascinating thing to see what happens not only to the children but to the paraprofessionals in this situation. We have a wealth of opportunity here.

When we got into this whole business of people, there was major emphasis upon the role of the parent. We have been rather arrogant, at times, as to the role of the parent in regard to his youngster's learning. It is true that, at times, we have suggested to the parent that the school and what goes on there really aren't of direct significance to him. Moore made the point that about a third of the learning is related to the home and the kind of reinforcement the youngster gets there.

I see the paraprofessional and the parent coming together, because not all homes are equipped to give the individualized attention that is significant for the learner. Use of the paraprofessional pays off in many situations. What we really are getting in these situations, whether in a good home or through the appropriate use of paraprofessionals, is highly qualified instruction. Someone really is listening to this child and relating to him as an individual, even if it is only for a few minutes a day.

This area has significance for the National Congress of Parents and Teachers. They can function in both of these roles in various situations. I have asked Mrs. Hendryson, President of the PTA, to ask her board to form a joint committee with our association to look into the whole matter of the role of the parent in reading instruction. The point is that the parents do have a role.

DOROTHY DIETRICH: The implication has been made that the present school systems sometimes do not meet the needs of all of their people. We have seen evidence that there are a number of outside programs, conducted by people who have no connection with the education establishment, that are doing an excellent job in helping others reach the level of literacy which will permit them to carry on in today's society. It follows that there are alternate ways of getting to individuals other than those of the established patterns.

We must, therefore, reevaluate the kinds of programs that are being carried out, and the kinds of things that are being done. There needs to be support for the programs that are being carried on outside the present school setup.

Another continuing aspect is the implication that a great deal needs to happen within the schools themselves. Time and time again we have heard about the identity of the individual; we have been asked what the end of education is. It seems to me that we need to carry to the teachers the messages that we have been hearing. We need to upgrade teacher education, preservice education. Some radical changes need to be made.

We must begin to think in terms of realistic goals for youngsters; we must begin to find other ways of imparting information. Reading is important. But there are other ways of "educating" some of these youngsters to tide them over. I am thinking particularly of those youngsters who have had problems in reading and who need other ways of acquiring information until we can help them with their reading problem.

I have been upset by hearing a statement made several times that learning does not take place until the child has begun to read. I don't think this statement is true. Reading is important. Reading must take place. But at the same time, it must be put in its proper perspective. We must realize that there are some youngsters who probably need to be given information and then, with a background of information, can be helped to learn to read.

Our responsibility now is to let teachers know that teaching reading is just as important today, if not more important, than it ever was and that all of us had better upgrade and uptool ourselves if we are going to prepare youngsters to live in a 1980 society.

VIRGINIA MATHEWS: I am sure you mean to imply also that it is not only important to teach the skills of reading but also the naturalness of reading and the self-identity made possible by reading.

DOROTHY DIETRICH: Yes, I think that sometimes we become lost in skills. We teach skills for the sake of teaching a skill. Again, what is the end of education? Why are we teaching reading? Unless each and every one of our teachers sees the goal of reading instruction as being personal enjoyment and the acquisition of information, not just today but throughout a lifetime, then we are losing sight of the goal of our instructional program.

It is a much broader thing than the first or second grade teacher would like to make it. The child who has not learned to read or does not read when he leaves twelfth grade indicates that we have failed as a school system. "We" means "each and every one of us." Somewhere along the line someone should have found a way to get to that youngster. We have too many youngsters leaving our schools at twelfth grade who use reading in a very limited way.

VIRGINIA MATHEWS: It is evident that we have a job to do now. We must find ways to convey the points that have been made here to some of the individuals and groups who must become aware of them.

One thread running through several of the discussions has not been mentioned specifically: that is, what Springs said about his high school and the paperback. There is a tremendous variety of paperbacks on the market for children to buy themselves, and the schools that make them available can hardly keep them stocked. The vital importance of access to a wide variety of books is something that perhaps has not been identified specifically, but was said to us a number of times. Greater access to books is one of the things that we should think about recommending.

Here, I have to put in a plug for libraries, and particularly for school libraries which are becoming real multimedia centers where books and other kinds of stimulating materials are made available. We need to think about the libraries in addition to the access provided through the home, through paperbacks, and through other means.